COLLECTOR'S
VALUE GUIDE™

Jeff Gordon®

Collector Handbook
and Price Guide

PREMIERE EDITION

SO-CCJ-902

JEFF GORDON®

This publication is not affiliated with Jeff Gordon®, Jeff Gordon, Inc., J.G. Motorsports, Inc., Hendrick Motorsports, General Motors Corporation, NASCAR® or any of their affiliates, subsidiaries, distributors or representatives. Any opinions expressed are solely those of the authors, and do not necessarily reflect those of Jeff Gordon®, Jeff Gordon, Inc., J.G. Motorsports, Inc., Hendrick Motorsports, General Motors Corporation or NASCAR®. Jeff Gordon® is a registered trademark of Jeff Gordon, Inc. The likeness of the #24 race car is a trademark of Hendrick Motorsports.

EDITORIAL

Managing Editor:	Jeff Mahony
Associate Editors:	Melissa A. Bennett
	Jan Cronan
	Gia C. Manalio
	Paula Stuckart
Contributing Editor:	Mike Micciulla
Assistant Editors:	Heather N. Carreiro
	Jennifer Filipek
	Joan C. Wheal
Editorial Assistants:	Jennifer Abel
	Timothy R. Affleck
	Beth Hackett
	Christina M. Sette
	Steven Shinkaruk

WEB (collectorbee.com)

Web Reporter:	Samantha Bouffard
Web Graphic Designer:	Ryan Falis

R&D

R&D Specialist:	Priscilla Berthiaume
R&D Graphic Designer:	Angi Shearstone

ART

Creative Director:	Joe T. Nguyen
Assistant Art Director:	Lance Doyle
Senior Graphic Designers:	Susannah C. Judd
	David S. Maloney
	Carole Mattia-Slater
	David Ten Eyck
Graphic Designers:	Jennifer J. Bennett
	Sean-Ryan Dudley
	Kimberly Eastman
	Marla B. Gladstone
	Melanie Gonzalez
	Caryn Johnson
	Jaime Josephiac
	Jim MacLeod
	Jeremy Maendel
	Chery-Ann Poudrier

PRODUCTION

Production Manager:	Scott Sierakowski
Product Development Manager:	Paul Rasid

ISBN 1-585-98070-6

CHECKERBEE™ and COLLECTOR'S VALUE GUIDE™ are trademarks of CheckerBee, Inc. Copyright © 2000 by CheckerBee, Inc.
All rights reserved. No part of this book may be reproduced or transmitted in any form or by any means, electronic or mechanical, including photocopying, recording, or by any information storage or retrieval system, without the written permission of the publisher.

CheckerBee PUBLISHING

306 Industrial Park Road
Middletown, CT 06457

www.collectorbee.com

Table Of Contents

COLLECTOR'S
VALUE GUIDE™

Introducing The Collector's Value Guide™

Welcome to the premiere edition of the Collector's Value Guide™ to Jeff Gordon collectibles! The 1990s have seen the sport of NASCAR explode in popularity, and Jeff Gordon is among the drivers most responsible for creating this new wave of excitement. Since bursting onto the scene in the Busch Series Grand National Division in 1991, Gordon's popularity has been evidenced by the appearance of his name and likeness on an endless number of products ranging from fishing lures to belt buckles!

Die-cast cars are arguably the most popular racing collectible on the market today. From the smallest 1:144-scale cars to the lifelike 1:18s, this Collector's Value Guide™ is your complete source for information about all of them. Whether you're a new fan or have been following Gordon since his days as a Ford driver, you will find what you're looking for in these pages. Look inside for other great features including:

- A Gordon biography and racing timeline
- A spotlight on Gordon's NASCAR rivals
- Values for helmets, duallies, transporters, pit wagons and more
- A look at all of Gordon's trading cards and their values
- An overview of other Gordon merchandise
- Fan stories from Gordon fans across the globe
- Care and display tips for your collection
- And much, much more!

Jeff Gordon® – Driven To Succeed

Visit a Winston Cup race on any given Sunday and you just might be witness to something special. Although the tracks and opponents are different each week, a familiar sight often unfolds. As the field of 43 mighty steel chariots speeds its way into the final lap, a rainbow-colored Chevrolet Monte Carlo can often be seen breaking from the pack and taking the checkered flag. In the winner's circle, a young, athletic man with movie-star good looks emerges from the car. His name is Jeff Gordon, and his road to Winston Cup success begins on the West Coast, far from the Southern superspeedways of Charlotte and Atlanta.

How It All Began

Jeff Gordon was born on August 4, 1971 in Vallejo, California to Will and Carol Gordon. His parents divorced when he was a small child and Carol later married John Bickford. It was Bickford who nurtured and encouraged Gordon's need for speed. The young boy was a regular sight in the neighborhood, racing his bike as fast as he could pedal it. He got his first taste of horsepower when Bickford introduced him to quarter midget race cars at the age of five. A mixture of hard work, sacrifice and natural ability made Gordon almost unbeatable in the quarter midget races. By 1979, he was already a national champion of the quarter midget division. He would eventually capture two more national championships in that division as well as four national go-cart class championships.

COLLECTOR'S
VALUE GUIDE™

His family could sense that Gordon was an especially gifted racer, and moved to Pittsboro, Indiana when Gordon was a teenager. Bickford knew that his stepson needed to be closer to a traditional hotbed of racing. It was in the Midwest that Gordon could race the

more powerful sprint cars without being hampered by the age restrictions that existed in the state of California.

Sprint cars may be funny-looking machines, but their size and power are nothing to joke about. These lightweight racers, with their 600- to 800-horsepower engines, will get a driver down the track in the blink of an eye. Gordon made the transition from midgets to sprint cars look easy. At the age of 16, he earned his racing license from the United States Auto Club. Although he was the youngest driver ever to have attained this privilege, he continued to rule the race tracks like a seasoned veteran. In some ways he *was* a veteran – he'd already been racing for 11 years!

He won the USAC Midget Series National Championship in 1990, and continued his winning ways with the USAC Silver Crown Division National Championship a year later. He had graduated from high school, and was at a crossroads. Where would his career take him next? Would he find a new home on the Indy circuit? Or would his passions be stirred by something else?

Busch Beginnings

Thoughts of stock cars had been dancing in his head, and Gordon decided to give one a test spin at NASCAR legend Buck Baker's driving school in Rockingham, North Carolina. It was love at first throttle. Once he got behind the wheel of a stock car, he never looked back.

Gordon may have been racing for almost as long as he'd been able to walk, but he was not quite ready for the big leagues yet. NASCAR drivers don't automatically start out in  the venerable Winston Cup Series. These young, hungry individuals face weekly challenges on the proving grounds of the Busch Series Grand National Division. Although Busch serves in many respects as a junior circuit to the Winston Cup, the racing is no less fast, thrilling or dangerous. Luckily for Gordon, he had a wise owner named Bill Davis behind him. Gordon drove a Ford back then – sponsored first by Outback Steakhouse, then later by Carolina Ford Dealers and Baby Ruth. In Gordon's first season of Busch racing, he racked up five finishes in the top five, including one pole.

When he made the jump to full-time Winston Cup racing in 1993, it was without Bill Davis, who couldn't quite get a team together in time for the season. Enter Rick Hendrick. The Hendrick Motorsports racing team had money, sponsor support and the belief that Gordon could be the next star of the sport. The success of Gordon, Rick Hendrick and crew chief Ray Evernham would defy everyone's greatest expectations and eventually launch the young driver into the stratosphere of superstardom.

The Wonder Boy Years

Things started simply in that Winston Cup rookie season of 1993. Gordon had 30 starts, and while he didn't win any races, he finished second twice, and posted five additional top-five finishes. His numbers were impressive enough that he was named the Winston Cup Rookie of the Year. The 1994 season built upon the successful foundation set down the previous year. Gordon earned his first Winston Cup victory at the Coca-Cola 600 at the Charlotte Motor Speedway. An even more impressive victory came at the Brickyard 400 that August. There, in front of his hometown Indiana crowd, he outmaneuvered Ernie Irvin to win the race. Jeff Gordon had proved that he could hold his own with the big boys of NASCAR.

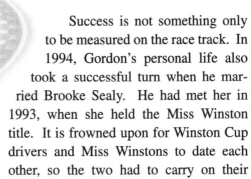

Jeff Gordon

Success is not something only to be measured on the race track. In 1994, Gordon's personal life also took a successful turn when he married Brooke Sealy. He had met her in 1993, when she held the Miss Winston title. It is frowned upon for Winston Cup drivers and Miss Winstons to date each other, so the two had to carry on their romance in secret. Today, they are one of the most recognized couples in NASCAR, with Brooke proving to be almost as popular a celebrity as her husband. Gordon is smart to listen to her advice. It was she who convinced him to shave off his moustache! Brooke's deep religious convictions have also influenced him. God is never far from Gordon's mind when he races because his wife selects a scripture verse for him to tape to his dashboard before each race.

Despite all of his career accomplishments thus far, nothing could have prepared Gordon for the banner year that 1995 turned out to be. His seven wins that year helped cement his lead in the Winston Cup points standings, and he beat out the rest of the pack to become the Winston Cup champion. Now that Gordon and Evernham had found their winning rhythm, more championships would follow.

Gordon did not win the Winston Cup championship in 1996, even though he posted a career-high 10 victories. Instead, the championship went to Hendrick teammate Terry Labonte. In 1997, however, Gordon would post numbers that no one could deny. That year he became the youngest driver to win the legendary Daytona 500. He also became only the second driver to be awarded the Winston Million. This award of $1 million in prize money goes to any driver

who can win at least three out of the four "crown jewel" races at Charlotte, Darlington, Daytona or Talladega. By season's end, Gordon had once again won 10 races. This time that number was good enough for him to be crowned Winston Cup champion.

By 1998, Gordon had become the man everyone wanted to beat. He responded to the pressure by winning 13 races, including a record four wins in a row. It seemed that Gordon had taken his team's motto, "Refuse to Lose," literally. Although more wins were around the corner for Gordon, his team would endure a potentially crippling blow in the coming year.

Dark Clouds Over The Rainbow

Gordon's 1999 racing campaign seemed poised to capture a third consecutive championship. Indeed, his seven wins that season were more than any of his competitors posted. The true turbulence that year came from within, when five members of Gordon's "Rainbow Warriors" pit crew left the Hendrick team for a rival team named Robert Yates Racing. A driver's pit crew is just as responsible for wins as the driver is, and the Rainbow Warriors made up one of the best. With that blow, Jeff Gordon's

COLLECTOR'S
VALUE GUIDE™

chances for another Winston Cup championship got sidelined in the pits.

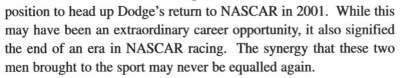

Even more stunning was Ray
Evernham's decision to resign his position
as crew chief before the season had even
ended. It had often seemed like nothing
could separate Gordon and his friend
and mentor, but Evernham accepted a
position to head up Dodge's return to NASCAR in 2001. While this
may have been an extraordinary career opportunity, it also signified
the end of an era in NASCAR racing. The synergy that these two
men brought to the sport may never be equalled again.

On The Rebound

If Jeff Gordon had been shaken by the surprising turn of events
in the 1999 season, it was difficult to tell. Under the direction of
interim crew chief Brian Whitesell, Gordon and the Rainbow
Warriors won their next two races in Martinsville and Charlotte.
Although the importance of Evernham should not be overlooked, it
was evident that Gordon had matured and gained confidence behind
the wheel over his eight seasons of professional racing. He was ready
to take a more active role in matters outside of the driver's seat.
Evernham's exit allowed Gordon to step up to the challenge of serv-
ing the Hendrick team in an even greater capacity.

Gordon's wins and endorse-
ment deals with sponsors such
as Pepsi and Kellogg's (just to
name a couple) have made him
a multi-millionaire. In just eight
seasons of Winston Cup driving,
Gordon has earned over $30 million.
He is such a popular advertising icon
that the money he makes for endorse-

ments is double that of his race earnings.

But Gordon has never been one to just take the money and run. He contributes much of his winnings to charity. He is also closely partnered with the Hendrick Marrow Program, an offshoot of The Marrow Foundation, which seeks bone marrow matches for leukemia patients. When he won the Winston Million, Gordon donated $100,000 of that bonus prize to The Marrow Foundation.

What The Future Holds

Gordon's bright racing prospects show no signs of dimming. His sponsor, DuPont, is partnered with him until 2005. He has also signed a lifetime agreement with Hendrick Motorsports, ensuring his status as not only a driver, but as a business partner as well. The new pit crew is beginning to gel, and Brian Whitesell has been promoted to the position of team manager. Robbie Loomis, a former crew chief for Richard Petty, has been brought in to become the Rainbow Warriors' new crew chief. In 2000, Gordon reached the milestone of 50 career wins, a feat no other driver has accomplished as quickly. If he can continue to win at the pace he set in the 1990s, NASCAR just might crown itself a new "king" for the new century!

Jeff Gordon®
Racing Timeline

1985   Jeff Gordon grows up in Vallejo, California, racing and winning against other children his own age. He makes the jump from go-carts to sprint cars.

1986   His family moves to Indiana in order to be closer to more racing opportunities. Although he's not old enough to drive a car, Gordon holds his own at Jacksonville's All Star Florida Speedweeks.

1987   Gordon races sprint cars in his World of Outlaws debut. National exposure follows after he is featured on ESPN's "Speedweeks" program.

1988   This is his final year in the World of Outlaws. He goes on to thrill audiences overseas in New Zealand, where he wins 14 out of 15 of his races there.

1989   Gordon wins the United States Auto Club's (USAC) Midget Rookie of the Year honors.

1990   Gordon claims victory in the USAC midget championship.

1991   Gordon becomes the youngest driver to win the USAC Silver Crown Division title. His fantastic good fortune continues when he is named Rookie of the Year in the Busch Series.

1992   Gordon races in his first Winston Cup start, which is also the final one for racing great Richard Petty.

1993 He wins his first Winston Cup pole. His two second-place finishes help earn him Winston Cup Rookie of the Year honors.

1994 Gordon experiences his first Winston Cup victory in the Coca-Cola 600 at Charlotte Motor Speedway. His second win comes just weeks later at the inaugural Brickyard 400.

1995 Gordon holds off the veterans to become the youngest Winston Cup champion of the modern era. His earnings for the year total more than $4 million.

1996 With 10 wins, Gordon has more wins than any other driver in the Winston Cup. He finishes second to Terry Labonte in the Winston Cup points standings.

1997 Gordon becomes the second driver ever to win the Winston Million bonus. He caps off his season by earning his second Winston Cup championship.

1998 Gordon's 13 wins tie the record set by Richard Petty in 1975. The season ends triumphantly when he is crowned the youngest three-time Winston Cup champion.

1999 Gordon wins seven races, including two from the pole position, on his way to a sixth-place finish in the Winston Cup points standings.

2000 On April 16, Gordon wins his 50th race. No other driver has ever earned 50 victories faster than Gordon.

A Look At
The Rainbow Warriors

No matter whom you have behind the wheel, a stock car could never finish a grueling 500-lap race without a talented pit crew in place. Luckily for Jeff Gordon, his squad of Rainbow Warriors is one of the best in the business. While many doubted that Gordon would make a full recovery after losing Ray Evernham as crew chief, the motto "Refuse to Lose" still serves as words to live by for the new and improved Rainbow Warriors.

What does a pit crew do that makes them so indispensible? And just what exactly is a gas man or catch-can man? Read on as we "jump the wall" and enter the fast-paced world of the pits.

An Off-The-Wall Job

Seven crew members are allowed in the pit box to work on a car. Once the car pulls into the pit box, the pit crew dashes over the wall to perform their duties. Each team member has a specialized task to perform. If each Rainbow Warrior completes his task flawlessly, aiming for a time of 20 seconds or less, Gordon can speed back into the race without losing his valuable positioning on the track. Pit crews that move slowly lose championships.

The jack man has one of the most important jobs in the pits. He uses a lightweight jack to elevate the car so that the old tires can be taken off and replaced with new ones. As he is doing this, the tire carriers relay new tires to the tire changers, who place them quickly and efficiently on the car.

The gas man is responsible for refueling the car. But unlike when you fill up your steel chariot at the local gas station, the gas man has to carry an 11-gallon gas can that tips the scales at almost 90 pounds. He does this not once, but twice during every pit stop. The catch-can man's job is linked to the gas man's job. When the car's gas tank is full, any excess fuel is caught in a container called a catch-can.

Once the car has been refueled with gas and refitted with tires, it speeds out of the pits and re-enters the race. No matter how well a pit crew does its job, it is only a matter of time before the car is back in the pit box, ready to be serviced again.

In addition to the Rainbow Warriors who man the pits, other members of the Rainbow Warriors team work hard behind the scenes both in the pit stall area behind the pit wall, and at the race shop to keep Gordon driving smoothly. For example, fabricators use sheet metal to prepare the body of the car and specialized mechanics make sure each and every one of the car's parts is in working order. One

of the unsung jobs of the Rainbow Warriors is that of the truck driver. Without the truck driver, the car would never make it to the racetrack!

The New Rainbow?

Much has been made in the press about Ray Evernham's departure and the loss of five Rainbow Warriors to the Robert Yates Racing team. The Rainbow Warriors have experienced an uncharacteristic period of highs and lows as they slowly rebuild team chemistry. But with Robbie Loomis and Brian Whitesell, the Hendrick Motorsports team has put the right men in place to guide the Rainbow Warriors into a new era of racing prosperity.

Robbie Loomis

The crew chief's job is one of strategic planning. Split-second decisions such as knowing whether to change two or four tires during a pit stop can often be the deciding factor in a race. Robbie Loomis's title of crew chief makes him the leader of the Rainbow Warriors. Loomis is no stranger to leadership positions. Before joining the Hendrick Motorsports team, Loomis served as a crew chief for Petty Enterprises. As one talented enough to serve the "king" of stock car racing, Loomis should do well heading up the sport's modern-day equivalent of racing royalty.

Brian Whitesell

Team manager Brian Whitesell is a multi-talented engineer who has been with the Hendrick Motorsports team since its inception. His long loyalty paid off when he was named the immediate replacement crew chief in place of the departing Ray Evernham. With Whitesell calling the shots, Gordon jumped out to back-to-back wins. Since the hiring of Robbie Loomis to the crew chief position, Whitesell is now responsible for maintaining the daily operation of the team. As someone who has been with the team since day one, no one is better suited to see it through its day-to-day trials and triumphs.

NASCAR® Overview

There's something innately appealing about a stock car race. While other forms of automobile racing may deliver faster thrills and higher speeds, the long-lasting allure of stock car racing has its roots in the appeal of the cars themselves. Who hasn't sat behind the wheel of a Ford Taurus, Chevrolet Monte Carlo or Pontiac Grand Prix while in congested highway traffic and envisioned piloting Rusty Wallace's, Jeff Gordon's or Tony Stewart's car down the straightaway at Lowe's Motor Speedway? It was only a half century ago that these cars were strictly stock models racing down dirt tracks in front of tiny, but appreciative, crowds.

Stock car racing's roots stretch back to the moonshiners and bootleggers who needed superior driving skills to avoid the authorities and transport their unlawful product throughout the rural southern United States. These daredevil drivers later found their skills useful in another thrilling avenue – stock car racing.

Automobile racing has been around for as long as there have been automobiles, but stock car racing attracted a breed of driver all its own. Not every driver was a bootlegger. Some were speed freaks and gear heads. Others were die-hard competitors. Most were just average individuals who liked to race their own cars for enjoyment and maybe win a small prize if they were lucky.

Many great successes result from the iron will and unyielding determination of a single visionary. Stock car racing had just such an individual to lead it through its formative years: Bill France.

Big Bill

William H.G. France left Washington, D.C. in the mid-1930s to settle with his wife in Daytona Beach, Florida. A mechanic and occasional auto racer, France found himself in the middle of a burgeoning racing movement that centered on Daytona Beach.

The picturesque Daytona Beach may have seemed an unlikely spot for racing, but race there they did, fighting wet sand and high tides in addition to the other racers. Racing at Daytona Beach had started before World War II, but it was the efforts of France that landed Daytona Beach – and stock car racing – on the map.

One of the problems facing early stock car racing was the lack of a unifying body to govern the sport. France saw that he could fill this void, and in late 1947, met with a mix of promoters, drivers and mechanics to form the National Association of Stock Car Auto Racing – NASCAR. France was named president, and wasted no time in exerting his power for the good of the sport.

NASCAR was a family enterprise from the very beginning. France's wife, Anne, played an important role in keeping the early association afloat financially. Anne's business skills served her well as NASCAR's secretary and treasurer. Besides Anne, several women played a vital role in NASCAR's early history. From key personnel in the front office to daring drivers on the racetrack, women excelled on all levels of the sport.

Starting with NASCAR's first season in 1948, large crowds were attracted to the dirt tracks of the southern United States throughout the late 1940s and 1950s. But if the sport was going to rise to new levels of popularity, "Big Bill" would need to succeed with a big idea he had brewing.

The Rise Of The Superspeedway

Small dirt tracks had been the norm in racing, but Bill France envisioned greater things. After several years and several million dollars, his 2.5-mile Daytona International Speedway became a reality in 1959. Built with the help of his International Speedway Corporation, this "super" speedway revolutionized every aspect of the sport.

Atlanta, California and North Carolina soon followed with impressive speedways of their own. France had once again changed the face of stock car racing. As more and more of these streamlined superspeedways sprang up, the sport began to streamline itself, also. All sorts of racing series had taken place under the umbrella of NASCAR, but the Grand National series emerged as the premier showcase. It was one driver in particular who would serve as the first superstar for this new era of racing.

King Richard And His Court

Richard Petty had followed in the footsteps of his father Lee to become a remarkable NASCAR driver. Lee had been a force in the early days of the Grand National, winning the first Daytona 500 and a total of three championships. In his 32-year career, Richard Petty expanded the Petty dynasty. Richard captured seven Winston Cup Championships, seven Daytona 500 victories and an astounding 200 career victories, including 27 wins in one season!

The exploits of Richard Petty were heightened by the colorful cast of drivers who battled the so-called king of racing for supremacy. David Pearson would prove to be Petty's main foil. Pearson, whose 105 career wins place him second only to Petty, would also capture three Winston Cup championships in a career that spanned over a quarter of a century. Pearson's greatest recognition came when he was selected as "Driver of the Century" by his fellow NASCAR associates in the pages of "Sports Illustrated."

Cale Yarborough and Bobby Allison were two other popular drivers of the time. Yarborough, who won 83 races in his Winston Cup career, also won an unprecedented three Winston Cup championships in a row. Allison, the winner of 84 races in his career, was also voted NASCAR's most popular driver six times. These two drivers' names remain inextricably linked after events brought the two men to blows at the conclusion of the 1979 Daytona 500, one of the wildest Daytona races of the modern era and the first to be covered from start to finish on live television.

The Modern Era

When reading through the NASCAR record book, the term "modern era" is often mentioned. The modern era was ushered in by Bill France, Jr. in 1972 when a new, shorter schedule was unveiled. Bill France, Jr. had taken the reins to NASCAR over from his father, and immediately set out to re-establish NASCAR's dominance in the world of stock car racing. The new, shorter schedule meant that teams no longer had to race throughout the country, multiple times a week. Fewer races a season, however, now make some of the older season records nearly untouchable. With a NASCAR season now only 34 races long, it is doubtful that any driver will ever again win 27 races in a single season.

Dollars And Sense

Bill France, Jr. has succeeded in increasing NASCAR's empire in ways his father could have only imagined. Under the younger France's leadership, NASCAR has become a multi-billion dollar enterprise. Television networks that were once leery of broadcasting lengthy races now hand over hundreds of millions of dollars to secure rights to air the races. Track attendance remains healthy at more than 10 million people each year and NASCAR has a television audience of more than 200 million viewers annually.

There's nothing "fair-weather" about these legions of NASCAR fanatics. NASCAR enjoys the highest brand loyalty of any sport. If Jeff Gordon is seen drinking a can of Pepsi in a television commercial, there's bound to be a six-pack of that same soda in the fridges and coolers of fans of the #24 car.

No matter how big NASCAR gets, it remains a close-knit, family affair. Bill France, Jr. continues in his father's footsteps as president, while brother Jim heads up the International Speedway Corporation, and Bill's son Brian serves his father in the role of senior vice president. The cars may be faster and the seasons may be shorter, but the sport remains true to the vision mapped out by "Big Bill" France in December of 1947.

COLLECTOR'S
VALUE GUIDE™

Anatomy Of A Race Car

Jeff Gordon's rainbow-colored DuPont car is known as a stock car. Stock cars have several special features and modifications that allow them to race and survive speeds of 200 miles per hour.

1. Roof flaps – Safety feature that flips up to prevent the car from becoming airborne in a crash.

2. Rear spoiler – Can be adjusted to produce varying amounts of resistance.

3. Car number – Allows easy identification of the car in a race.

4. Windshield – Made of lexan, the same plastic used for windshields on fighter jets.

5. Primary sponsor – Primary sponsors have been known to pay more than $5 million to have their name and colors featured on a car.

6. Window net – A safety feature that prevents drivers from being thrown out of the car.

7. Tires – Racing tires are treadless in order to provide the driver with more traction on the road.

8. Exhaust – Pipes are located under the driver's side window.

9. Arrow – Designates where to position the jack during pit stops.

10. **Headlights** – These aren't really headlights at all. Headlights are unnecessary and a potential glass hazard, so decals are placed there instead.

11. **Grill opening** – Allows air to reach the radiator and brakes.

12. **Model name** – Car models currently being raced are the Chevrolet Monte Carlo, Ford Taurus and Pontiac Grand Prix. Dodge Intrepid joins the cars on the racetrack in 2001.

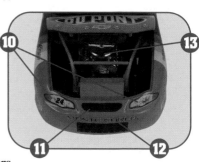

13. **Engine** – Winston Cup cars use an eight-cylinder engine similar to the one found in a typical car. Unlike a regular engine, however, Winston Cup engines have been modified to have a much larger engine block that can produce significantly greater horsepower.

14. **Fuel cell** – Located in the trunk, it serves the same purpose as a regular car's gas tank. Stock cars use a specially produced 110-octane gasoline.

15. **Taillights** – As with the headlights, stock car taillights are just decals placed over where the real thing would go.

16. **Cooling system** – Circulates air from outside of the car onto the driver through his helmet and the holes in his seat. Keeps temperatures from becoming unbearable on hot days.

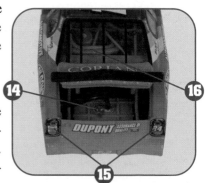

Rivals Of The Road

The world of NASCAR is often described in terms of a family. As with any family, there are bound to be squabbles and rivalries. Although fans of competing racers may play up certain rivalries between drivers, those grudges are  often exaggerated and blown out of proportion. That doesn't mean that the drivers are immune to flared tempers and dented fenders. While each driver has a good chance of winning any given race, the following drivers are ones that Jeff Gordon probably does not want to see bearing down on him in the final lap.

Jeff Burton

There's more than one Jeff turning heads in the Winston Cup. Jeff Burton was named the Winston Cup Rookie of the Year the year following Gordon, and while Burton has not yet equalled Gordon's success on the track, he has claimed some very impressive wins. When the two Jeffs went head to head at the 1998 Exide NASCAR Select Batteries 400 at Richmond International Raceway, it was Burton who won the checkered flag. The two have also battled it out at Darlington Raceway. The most publicized battle between the Gordon and Burton teams came when Burton's team owner Jack Roush accused the Gordon camp of cheating. One thing is for certain: When Burton and Gordon go head to head, race fans hungry for excitement are never cheated.

Dale Earnhardt

"The Intimidator." "The Man In Black." Whatever the nickname, Dale Earnhardt continues to be one of the most fearsome opponents in Winston Cup racing. Earnhardt has been racing in the Winston Cup Series for a quarter  of a century, and in that time has achieved some incredible numbers. He is the only driver to be named Rookie of the Year and then win a Winston Cup championship in the same year. His seven Winston Cup championships tie him with the legendary Richard Petty, and an eighth championship would give Earnhardt sole possession of the all-time record. Gordon and Earnhardt's most famous clash came at the 1997 Daytona 500, when Gordon sent Earnhardt crashing into the turn wall. While crashes are an inevitable part of racing, it's incidents like that one that fuel the rivalry between Earnhardt and Gordon fans, making it one of the strongest rivalries in sports.

Dale Earnhardt, Jr.

If there's any truth to the saying "like father, like son," the Earnhardt family will continue to be a thorn in Jeff Gordon's side well into this new millennium. Gordon and "Little E" first competed against each other on the Busch circuit in 1999. Veteran driver Gordon had been competing in Busch races that year to hone his skills, and these skills were tested to their limit against the up-and-coming Earnhardt, Jr. in Michigan's NAPA 200. Earnhardt Jr., the 1998 and 1999 Busch Series champion, proved unstoppable even for the seasoned driver Gordon. "Little E" may have won that Busch battle, but the Winston Cup war is now just beginning and far from over.

COLLECTOR'S
VALUE GUIDE™

Tony Stewart

The story is a familiar one. A young driver who gets his start in go-carts, midgets and sprint cars and moves up the Busch ladder, eventually taking the world of Winston by storm, earning Rookie of the Year honors. Sound familiar? While these words describe Jeff Gordon, they also apply to the phenomenal Tony Stewart. Before joining NASCAR, Stewart's career took a brief detour into Indy racing, where he was named the 1996 Indianapolis 500 Rookie of the Year. Stewart was an easy choice for Rookie of the Year honors in the Winston Cup Series also, where his three victories in 1999 were the most ever for a rookie driver. With such similar and evenly matched racing backgrounds, it wouldn't be surprising if Stewart and Gordon one day raced to a tie.

Rusty Wallace

You can't judge a book by its cover, and you can't judge a racer by his name. Rusty's driving is anything *but* rusty, and this sharp driver can often be found locking horns with Jeff Gordon as the two men vie for first place during a race. While their cars have traded paint in the past, the 1998 Pontiac Excitement 400 at Richmond International Speedway saw the two men trade words as well, after Wallace's #2 Ford sent the #24 Chevy into the wall in the second turn. NASCAR championships are not won by words alone, but Rusty continues to put his motor where his mouth is as he competes for his second Winston Cup championship.

Facts On The Tracks

Early NASCAR racetracks were little more than well-worn dirt tracks that were laid out and practiced on by bootleggers and moonshiners in the southern United States. Today, NASCAR racetracks can be found from coast to coast. These gleaming structures may have luxury suites and 100,000-fan capacity, but they are not far removed from those simpler tracks of yesteryear. In fact, many early tracks are still being raced on today. Different drivers perform better on different tracks, so the variety of tracks ensures a dynamic season of racing. The following are some of the most noteworthy tracks, listed alphabetically by state. See you at the race!

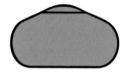

Talladega, AL

Talladega Superspeedway is a 2.66- mile, oval-shaped track with 33-degree banking. Talladega can seat 108,000 and accommodate even more in the 215-acre infield.

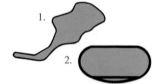

Phoenix, AZ

Phoenix International Raceway features a 1-mile, oval-shaped track with 11 degrees of banking. This raceway is known as the "Desert Mile."

1. Sonoma, CA
2. Fontana, CA

1. Sears Point Raceway is a 1.949-mile track with an 11-turn course.

2. California Speedway features a 2-mile oval-shaped track with 14-degree banking.

1.

2.

Dover, DE

Dover Downs International Speedway is known to NASCAR fans as "The Monster Mile." It seats more than 107,000and features a 1-mile oval-shaped track with 24-degree banking.

COLLECTOR'S
VALUE GUIDE™

1. Daytona Beach, FL
2. Homestead, FL

1. Daytona International Speedway is 2.5 miles long and features 31-degree banking.

2. Homestead-Miami Speedway is a 1.5-mile track with 8 degrees of banking.

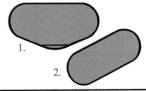

Hampton, GA

Atlanta Motor Speedway, located in Hampton, Georgia, is a 1.54-mile oval track with 24-degree banking. This speedway is accompanied by 330 acres of additional facilities, such as tennis courts.

Speedway, IN

Indianapolis Motor Speedway is a 2.5- mile, oval-shaped track with 9-degree banking. It is known to NASCAR fans as "The Brickyard" because it was originally paved with 3.2 million bricks.

Sparta, KY

Kentucky Speedway is a brand-new motorsports facility. It is the only speedway to be opened in the year 2000. The 1.5-mile tri-oval racetrack with 14-degree banking is a multi-million dollar marvel.

Brooklyn, MI

Michigan Speedway is over 30 years old, but fans love this 2-mile track with 18-degree banking because there is a view of the entire track from just about every seat in the complex.

Las Vegas, NV

Las Vegas Motor Speedway has a 1.5- mile, oval-shaped track with 12-degree banking. Known as the "Diamond in the Desert," it attracts race fans who are in search of a NASCAR oasis.

Loudon, NH

New Hampshire International Speedway features a 1-mile, oval-shaped track with 12-degree banking. Fifty acres of parking have recently been added to the facility to accommodate the large crowds drawn in by the races each year.

Facts On The Tracks

Watkins Glen, NY

Watkins Glen International features a 2.45-mile road course, with seven right-turn corners within its 11 corners. In 1998, this speedway celebrated its 50th anniversary, along with NASCAR.

1. Concord, NC
2. Rockingham, NC

1. Lowe's Motor Speedway is a 1.5-mile track with 24-degree banking.

2. North Carolina Speedway features a 1- mile, oval-shaped track with 22-degree banking.

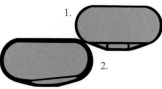

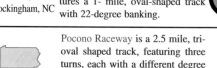

Long Pond, PA

Pocono Raceway is a 2.5 mile, tri-oval shaped track, featuring three turns, each with a different degree of banking. Adding to the excitement are three straightaways of varying lengths.

Darlington, SC

Darlington Raceway features a 1.366- mile track, with 23- to 25-degree banking. Darlington is the first superspeedway of NASCAR and is known to many fans and drivers as "Too Tough To Tame."

Bristol, TN

Bristol Motor Speedway features a 0.5-mile oval-shaped track with 36-degree banking. This raceway is known to many race fans as "The World's Fastest Half-Mile."

Fort Worth, TX

Texas Motor Speedway ranks as the second-largest sports facility in the United States. This speedway features a 1.5-mile oval-shaped track with 24-degree banking.

1. Richmond, VA
2. Ridgeway, VA

1. Richmond International Raceway has a 0.75-mile oval-shaped track with 14-degree banking.

2. Martinsville Speedway has a 0.526-mile oval-shaped track with 12-degree banking. The complex covers more than 300 acres.

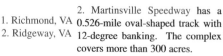

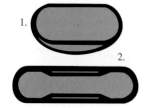

Top Five Cars

The following section lists the top-five most valuable Jeff Gordon die-cast cars.

Baby Ruth
1992 Ford Thunderbird
Racing Champions
1:24 scale
Value: $830

Baby Ruth
1992 Ford Thunderbird
Revell For RCI
1:24 scale
Value: $500

Chroma Premier
1997 Chevrolet Monte Carlo
Action/RCCA Elite
1:24 scale
Value: $420

DuPont
1997 Chevrolet Monte Carlo
Action/RCCA Elite
1:24 scale
Value: $355

ChromaLusion
1998 Chevrolet Monte Carlo
Action/RCCA Elite
1:24 scale
Value: $350

How To Use Your Collector's Value Guide™

1. Locate your die-cast piece. Cars begin on page 35, while other Jeff Gordon die-cast pieces, such as banks and suburbans, begin on page 65. Pieces are listed chronologically by their model year. For each piece is a listing of every manufacturer that produced it, listed in alphabetical order. Next to one manufacturer you will see a red triangle that indicates the manufacturer of the piece shown. (Please note that some of the photos are of the car in its box and that boxes

do vary from manufacturer to manufacturer.) Space is given for you in the LE column to record any limited edition information about your piece. Blank lines are also provided for you to add special pieces or future releases.

2. Record how many of each piece you have in the "How Many" box. Add up all of the values for each piece you have, and record that number in the "Total Value" box. Those die-cast products that have yet to register a secondary market value are identified as "N/E" (not established). Use the "Notes" box to record any information that will help you keep track of your collection. Now add up all of the "Total Value" boxes and record this value in the "Page Totals" box found at the bottom of each page. Do the same with your "How Many" totals.

3. Calculate the value for your entire collection by entering the values from the "Page Totals" boxes onto the corresponding lines of the "Total Value Of My Collection" section found on pages 125 and 126. When you total these numbers up, you will know the grand total of your complete collection!

1985

Although most people are familiar with Jeff Gordon's famous Winston Cup die-cast cars, replicas from Gordon's days as a midget and sprint car driver, dating back to 1985, are available from a variety of die-cast collectibles companies as well. So whether you just discovered Gordon yesterday, or have been a fan of his from the start, you are sure to find an amazing array of die-cast cars to choose from that will set your pulse racing!

Hap's
1985 Sprint

	Scale	LE	Value		Scale	LE	Value
❑ Action ▲	1:24		$160	❑			
❑				❑			

How Many:	Total Value:	Notes:

Yellow Sprint
1985 Sprint

	Scale	LE	Value		Scale	LE	Value
❏ Racing Champions	1:24		$135	❏			
❏ Racing Champions	1:64		$45	❏			
❏ Winner's Circle ▲	1:64		$43	❏			

How Many: **Total Value:**   **Notes:**

COLLECTOR'S
VALUE GUIDE™

1987

By the time Jeff Gordon was only 16 years old, he had already taken the world of sprint car racing by storm. Even then, he exhibited the poise and skill of a true champion. Die-cast reproductions of Gordon's 1987 Challenger sprint car remain in high demand with collectors. The #40 Challenger sprint is one of the most highly sought after in the 1:24 scale versions, but the 1:64 models by Action and Winner's Circle are also valued.

1

Challenger
1987 Sprint

	Scale	LE	Value		Scale	LE	Value
☐ Action ▲	1:24		$200	☐			
☐ Action	1:64		$18	☐			
☐ Winner's Circle Lifetime				☐			
Series	1:64		$38	☐			

How Many: **Total Value:**   **Notes:**

1988

Fans of Jeff Gordon know that he showed early promise driving quarter midget and sprint cars. In 1988, when he was 17 years old, Gordon was racing in the World of Outlaws sprint car series, where he competed against the nation's premier drivers. That same year also saw him competing in New Zealand, with continued success. Die-cast manufacturer GMP commemorated that winning year with a reproduction of Gordon's Molds Unlimited sprint car.

1

Molds Unlimited
1988 Sprint

	Scale	LE	Value			Scale	LE	Value
☐ GMP ▲	1:18		$290	☐				
☐				☐				

How Many:	Total Value:		Notes:	

Page Totals:	How Many	Total Value

COLLECTOR'S
VALUE GUIDE™

1990

Collectors who crave reproductions of the cars that Jeff Gordon drove in 1990 can take their pick from two very different machines. That year he won the U.S. Auto Club Midget Series National Championship, in which he drove the Diet Pepsi midget racer. That year also saw his entrance into the world of NASCAR Busch Series racing. Collectors who favor full-size stock car racing will enjoy the die-cast reproductions of the Outback Steakhouse Grand Prix, Gordon's first NASCAR entry.

1

Diet Pepsi
1990 Midget

	Scale	LE	Value		Scale	LE	Value
❑ Action Xtreme Series ▲	1:24		N/E	❑			
❑ Winner's Circle Lifetime Series	1:64		N/E	❑			
				❑			

How Many: **Total Value:**   **Notes:**

COLLECTOR'S
VALUE GUIDE™

	Page Totals:	How Many	Total Value

1990

Outback Steakhouse
1990 Pontiac Grand Prix

	Scale	LE	Value
❑ Action/RCCA ▲	1:64		N/E
❑ Action/RCCA Elite	1:24		N/E
❑ Winner's Circle Lifetime Series	1:64		N/E
❑			

	Scale	LE	Value
❑			
❑			

Note: The Outback Steakhouse car was Gordon's first entry into the world of stock car racing. He drove it in his first year of Busch Series competition.

How Many: | **Total Value:** | **Notes:**

1991

For fans familiar with seeing Jeff Gordon behind the wheel of a Chevrolet, the die-cast cars of 1991 may come as a surprise. Gordon was actually sponsored by Carolina Ford Dealers, driving a 1991 Ford Thunderbird! His keen driving in the Carolina Ford Dealers car earned him the 1991 Rookie of the Year title in the Busch Series. Although he did not win any races, his several second-place and top-five finishes gave race fans a glimpse of Gordon's future.

1

Carolina Ford
1991 Ford Thunderbird

	Scale	LE	Value		Scale	LE	Value
❑ Action	1:24		$92	❑ Winner's Circle	1:64		$16
❑ Action	1:64		$18	❑			
❑ Action/RCCA	1:64		$30	❑			
❑ Action/RCCA Elite ▲	1:24		$190	❑			
❑ Action/RCCA Elite SelectNet	1:24		N/E				

Note: Gordon won the Busch Rookie of the Year title after a strong season driving this car.

How Many:	Total Value:	Notes:

1992

One of the most popular die-cast cars from Jeff Gordon's 1992 racing campaign was the Baby Ruth Ford Thunderbird. This Busch Series car is available in four different scales. In 1992, for the first time, he also sat behind the wheel of a DuPont Chevrolet Lumina – a model he would go on to drive in 1993 and 1994. Gordon only saw limited action on the Winston Cup circuit that year, and his one Winston Cup start resulted in a "did not finish."

1

Baby Ruth
1992 Ford Thunderbird

	Scale	LE	Value		Scale	LE	Value
☐ Action	1:24		$75	☐ Racing Champions	1:24		$830
☐ Action	1:64		$17	☐ Racing Champions	1:43		$100
☐ Action/RCCA	1:64		$38	☐ Racing Champions	1:64		$115
☐ Action/RCCA by Revell	1:64		$80	☐ Revell for RCI	1:24		$500
☐ Action/RCCA Elite ▲	1:24		$190	☐ Winner's Circle			
☐ Ertl	1:18		$140	Lifetime Series	1:64		$17
☐ Matchbox/White Rose				☐			
Super Stars (orange)	1:64		$42	☐			
☐ Matchbox/White Rose				☐			
Super Stars (red)	1:64		$35	☐			

How Many: **Total Value:**   **Notes:**

Page Totals:	How Many	Total Value

DuPont
1992 Chevrolet Lumina

	Scale	LE	Value			Scale	LE	Value
☐ Winner's Circle Lifetime				☐				
Series ▲	1:64		N/E	☐				
☐								

Note: Gordon only drove in one Winston Cup race in 1992.

How Many:	Total Value:	Notes:

1993

1993

The die-cast cars that celebrate Jeff Gordon's 1993 Winston Cup season are a testament to his electrifying performance in his rookie season. Gordon did not win any races in 1993, but he did win his first pole – a great accomplishment for any young driver. He went on to win the Winston Cup Series Rookie of the Year title, a feat recognized by Matchbox/White Rose and Racing Champions, who released die-cast cars in recognition of his triumph.

1

DuPont
1993 Chevrolet Lumina

	Scale	LE	Value		Scale	LE	Value
❑ Matchbox/White Rose				❑ Racing Champions			
Super Stars	1:64		$16	(PVC Box)	1:64		$45
❑ Racing Champions ▲	1:24		$150	❑ Winner's Circle Lifetime			
❑ Racing Champions	1:43		$32	Series	1:64		$17
❑ Racing Champions	1:64		$48	❑			
❑ Racing Champions Premier	1:43		$75	❑			
❑ Racing Champions Premier	1:64		$100	❑			
❑ Racing Champions				❑			
Premier (1st Pole)	1:64		N/E	❑			

How Many: **Total Value:**   **Notes:**

Page Totals:	How Many	Total Value

COLLECTOR'S
VALUE GUIDE™

DuPont – Daytona 500
1993 Chevrolet Lumina

	Scale	LE	Value		Scale	LE	Value
❑ Racing Champions				❑			
(PVC Box) ▲	1:64		$45	❑			
❑				❑			

How Many:	Total Value:	Notes:

3

DuPont – Rookie Of The Year
1993 Chevrolet Lumina

	Scale	LE	Value		Scale	LE	Value
❑ Matchbox/White Rose				❑			
Super Stars	1:64		$18	❑			
❑ Racing Champions				❑			
Premier ▲	1:64		$100				
❑							

Note: Gordon's two second-place finishes helped him capture Winston Cup Rookie of the Year honors in 1993.

How Many:	Total Value:	Notes:

1994

In 1994, Jeff Gordon exhibited more brilliance, proving that he was a rising star in the world of stock car racing. On May 29, he earned his first Winston Cup win at the Coca-Cola 600. Racing Champions marked this occasion with 1:24 and 1:64 scale replicas of his Coca-Cola 600 car. Gordon's other win for the year came at the inaugural Brickyard 400 event, held at the Indianapolis Motor Speedway. Racing Champions honored this triumph with four die-cast versions of Gordon's Brickyard 400 car.

1

DuPont
1994 Chevrolet Lumina

	Scale	LE	Value		Scale	LE	Value
❑ Action	1:64		$50	❑ Racing Champions Premier	1:43		$45
❑ Action/RCCA	1:64		$86	❑ Racing Champions Premier	1:64		$85
❑ Matchbox/White Rose				❑ Racing Champions To			
Super Stars	1:64		$15	The Maxx	1:64		$40
❑ Racing Champions				❑ Racing Champions			
(with Snickers)	1:24		$90	(yellow box)	1:64		$45
❑ Racing Champions				❑ Revell ▲	1:24		$115
(without Snickers)	1:24		$135	❑ Winner's Circle Lifetime			
❑ Racing Champions	1:43		$60	Series	1:64		$14
❑ Racing Champions	1:64		$48	❑			
❑ Racing Champions				❑			
(Fan Club/PVC Box)	1:64		N/E	❑			

How Many:	Total Value:	Notes:

Page Totals:	How Many	Total Value

COLLECTOR'S VALUE GUIDE™

2

**PHOTO
UNAVAILABLE**

DuPont – Brickyard 400 Winner
1994 Chevrolet Lumina

	Scale	LE	Value		Scale	LE	Value
☐ Racing Champions	1:24		$110	☐			
☐ Racing Champions	1:64		$40	☐			
☐ Racing Champions Premier	1:43		$90	☐			
☐ Racing Champions Premier	1:64		$125	☐			

How Many: **Total Value:**   **Notes:**

3

DuPont – Coca-Cola 600 Winner
1994 Chevrolet Lumina

	Scale	LE	Value		Scale	LE	Value
☐ Racing Champions ▲	1:24		$155	☐			
☐ Racing Champions	1:64		$95	☐			
☐							
☐							

Note: Gordon's first Winston Cup win came driving this car in the Coca-Cola 600 on May 29, 1994.

How Many: **Total Value:**   **Notes:**

COLLECTOR'S
VALUE GUIDE™

Page Totals:	How Many	Total Value

1995

While the early years of Jeff Gordon's career had been filled with many high points, 1995 found him reaching the highest peak of all. Gordon's first Winston Cup championship increased his visibility, and several Gordon die-cast cars were released as a result. There are more than 15 different replicas of Gordon's 1995 Monte Carlo alone! Action also made a pewter version of this car available for collectors seeking an elegant touch to their collections.

1

DuPont
1995 Chevrolet Monte Carlo

	Scale	LE	Value
☐ Action	1:64		$23
☐ Action/RCCA ▲	1:24		$200
☐ Action/RCCA	1:64		$40
☐ Ertl (Buck Fever)	1:18		$135
☐ Ertl (By GMP)	1:18		$140
☐ Matchbox/White Rose Super Stars	1:64		$13
☐ Racing Champions	1:18		$90
☐ Racing Champions	1:24		$80
☐ Racing Champions	1:64		$34
☐ Racing Champions (Fan Club/PVC Box)	1:64		N/E
☐ Racing Champions Matched Serial Numbers	1:64		$36
☐ Racing Champions Premier	1:64		$45
☐ Racing Champions (Winston Cup Champ)	1:18		$115

	Scale	LE	Value
☐ Racing Champions (Winston Cup Champ)	1:24		$100
☐ Racing Champions Premier (Winston Cup Champ)	1:24		$110
☐ Racing Champions Premier (Winston Cup Champ)	1:64		$17
☐ Racing Champions Signature Series	1:18		$95
☐ Racing Champions Signature Series	1:24		$86
☐ Racing Champions Signature Series	1:64		$40
☐ Racing Champions Signature Series (hood open)	1:24		$98
☐ Racing Champions To The Maxx	1:64		$22
☐ Revell	1:24		$78

How Many: Total Value: Notes:

Page Totals:	How Many	Total Value

DuPont
1995 Chevrolet Monte Carlo

	Scale	LE	Value		Scale	LE	Value
☐ Action Pewter ▲	1:43		$145	☐			
☐				☐			

How Many:	Total Value:	Notes:

1996

Although Jeff Gordon didn't win the Winston Cup championship in 1996, his impressive total of 10 victories definitely caused his popularity to rise. Action, Matchbox/White Rose, Racing Champions and Revell all produced die-cast editions of his rainbow-colored 1996 DuPont car. Racing Champions even released a special chrome car. Whether you prefer a miniature 1:144 scale or a hefty 1:24 scale, there's sure to be a die-cast piece based on Gordon's 1996 car available in your preferred size and budget.

1

DuPont
1996 Chevrolet Monte Carlo

	Scale	LE	Value
❏ Action	1:64		$20
❏ Action/RCCA ▲	1:24		$120
❏ Action/RCCA	1:64		$50
❏ Matchbox/White Rose Super Stars	1:64		$10
❏ Matchbox/White Rose Super Star Awards	1:64		$40
❏ Racing Champions	1:24		$80
❏ Racing Champions	1:64		$35
❏ Racing Champions	1:144		$35
❏ Racing Champions Premier	1:64		$23

	Scale	LE	Value
❏ Racing Champions Preview	1:24		$68
❏ Racing Champions Preview	1:64		$30
❏ Racing Champions Promo (Unocal pack)	1:64		$42
❏ Racing Champions (PVC Box/Fan Club)	1:64		N/E
❏ Revell	1:24		$55
❏ Revell	1:64		$14
❏ Revell Collection	1:24		$75
❏			

Note: Gordon drove his 1996 DuPont Monte Carlo to ten wins in the 1996 season.

How Many: **Total Value:**   **Notes:**

Page Totals:	How Many	Total Value

PHOTO UNAVAILABLE

DuPont
1996 Chevrolet Monte Carlo

	Scale	LE	Value		Scale	LE	Value
☐ Racing Champions				☐			
Chrome Chase ▲	1:64		$275	☐			
☐				☐			

How Many:	Total Value:	Notes:

1997

In 1997, specially painted race cars became almost as familiar a sight as Jeff Gordon's traditional rainbow-colored die-cast models. DuPont unveiled its black and gold Chroma Premier paint scheme, and Gordon roared around the race track in a "Jurassic Park"-themed car, which promoted the "Jurassic Park – The Ride" attraction at Universal Studios Hollywood. Additionally, several manufacturers released a Million Dollar Date car commemorating Gordon's winning of the Winston Million bonus.

1

Chroma Premier
1997 Chevrolet Monte Carlo

	Scale	LE	Value		Scale	LE	Value
☐ Action	1:24		$190	☐ Winner's Circle	1:24		$42
☐ Action	1:64		$33	☐ Winner's Circle Lifetime			
☐ Action/RCCA	1:24		$300	Series	1:64		$24
☐ Action/RCCA	1:64		$60	☐			
☐ Action/RCCA Elite ▲	1:24		$420	☐			

How Many: **Total Value:** **Notes:**

Page Totals:	How Many	Total Value

COLLECTOR'S
VALUE GUIDE™

2

DuPont
1997 Chevrolet Monte Carlo

	Scale	LE	Value		Scale	LE	Value
❑ Action ▲	1:24		$82	❑ Racing Champions			
❑ Action (Brickyard 400)	1:24		$72	(Fan Club/PVC Box)	1:64		N/E
❑ Action (Brickyard 400)	1:64		$17	❑ Racing Champions Premier			
❑ Action/RCCA	1:64		$35	Preview	1:64		$25
❑ Action/RCCA Elite	1:24		$355	❑ Racing Champions Preview	1:24		$65
❑ Action/ RCCA Elite	1:64		$24	❑ Racing Champions Preview	1:64		$18
❑ Racing Champions	1:24		$75	❑ Winner's Circle	1:24		$35
❑ Racing Champions	1:64		$25	❑ Winner's Circle	1:64		$15
❑ Racing Champions	1:144		$22	❑			

How Many:	Total Value:	Notes:

3

Jurassic Park
1997 Chevrolet Monte Carlo

	Scale	LE	Value		Scale	LE	Value
❑ Action/RCCA	1:24		$188	❑ Winner's Circle Lifetime			
❑ Action/RCCA	1:64		$50	Series	1:64		$22
❑ Action/RCCA Elite ▲	1:24		$325	❑			
❑ Winner's Circle	1:24		$52	❑			

How Many:	Total Value:	Notes:

	How Many	Total Value
Page Totals:		

Million Dollar Date
1997 Chevrolet Monte Carlo

	Scale	LE	Value		Scale	LE	Value
☐ Action	1:64		$22	☐ Winner's Circle Lifetime			
☐ Action (black window)	1:64		$22	Series	1:24		$40
☐ Action/RCCA ▲	1:24		$140	☐ Winner's Circle Lifetime			
☐ Action/RCCA	1:64		$35	Series	1:64		$16
☐ Action/RCCA Elite	1:24		$200	☐			

How Many:	Total Value:	Notes:

Page Totals:	How Many	Total Value

1998

Jeff Gordon won an impressive 13 races in 1998 on his way to a third Winston Cup championship. NASCAR also celebrated its 50th anniversary in 1998, and Gordon's special ChromaLusion car marked this occasion on its hood. Action, Revell and Winner's Circle all produced Gordon cars in 1998. In addition to their standard releases, Action and Revell also honored Gordon's 1998 Brickyard 400 win, while Winner's Circle manufactured a die-cast car commemorating Gordon's status as a Winston Cup champion.

1

ChromaLusion
1998 Chevrolet Monte Carlo

	Scale	LE	Value		Scale	LE	Value
☐ Action ▲	1:24		$120	☐ Revell Collection	1:43		$60
☐ Action	1:64		$38	☐ Revell Collection	1:64		$38
☐ Action/RCCA	1:64		$65	☐ Revell Collection Club	1:18		$215
☐ Action/RCCA Elite	1:24		$350	☐ Revell Collection Club	1:24		$200
☐ Revell Collection	1:18		$150	☐			
☐ Revell Collection	1:24		$125	☐			

How Many:	Total Value:	Notes:

Page Totals:	How Many	Total Value

2

DuPont
1998 Chevrolet Monte Carlo

	Scale	LE	Value
❑ Action	1:24		$82
❑ Action	1:64		$18
❑ Action (Brickyard 400)	1:24		$140
❑ Action (Brickyard 400)	1:64		$17
❑ Action/RCCA	1:64		$25
❑ Action/RCCA Elite	1:24		$250
❑ Revell Collection	1:18		$135
❑ Revell Collection ▲	1:24		$78
❑ Revell Collection	1:43		$45
❑ Revell Collection	1:64		$16
❑ Revell Collection (Brickyard 400)	1:24		$90
❑ Revell Collection (Brickyard 400)	1:64		$16
❑ Revell Collection Club	1:18		$220

	Scale	LE	Value
❑ Revell Collection Club	1:24		$215
❑ Revell Select	1:24		$52
❑ Revell Select	1:64		$13
❑ Winner's Circle	1:24		$32
❑ Winner's Circle	1:43		$17
❑ Winner's Circle	1:64		$13
❑ Winner's Circle (Winston Cup Champ)	1:64		$11
❑ Winner's Circle Lifetime Series NASCAR 50th Anniversary (Wal-Mart exclusive)	1:64		N/E
❑			

Note: Gordon's 13 wins in 1998 tied the modern record.

How Many:	Total Value:	Notes:

3

DuPont
1998 Chevrolet Monte Carlo

	Scale	LE	Value		Scale	LE	Value
❑ Action/RCCA 24K Gold ▲	1:32		$88	❑			
❑				❑			

How Many:	Total Value:	Notes:

Page Totals:	How Many	Total Value

COLLECTOR'S
VALUE GUIDE™

4

PHOTO
UNAVAILABLE

DuPont – Fan Club
1998 Chevrolet Monte Carlo

	Scale	LE	Value		Scale	LE	Value
☐ Action/RCCA ▲	1:64		N/E	☐			
☐				☐			

How Many:	Total Value:	Notes:

5

DuPont – No Bull
1998 Chevrolet Monte Carlo

	Scale	LE	Value		Scale	LE	Value
☐ Action ▲	1:24		$85	☐ Action/RCCA Elite	1:24		$210
☐ Action	1:64		$17	☐			
☐ Action/RCCA	1:64		$36	☐			

How Many:	Total Value:	Notes:

Page Totals:	How Many	Total Value

1999

Jeff Gordon returned to his Busch Series roots in 1999 behind the wheel of a Pepsi-emblazoned Chevrolet Monte Carlo. The same year, the Force was with him when he raced a special "Star Wars: Episode 1" car, also in the Busch Series. Gordon also drove exciting paint schemes in his Winston Cup races. The popular cartoon "NASCAR Racers" was represented, as well as Superman! As a member of the Superman Racing team, Gordon joined forces with some of the greatest names in auto racing.

1

DuPont
1999 Chevrolet Monte Carlo

	Scale	LE	Value		Scale	LE	Value
☐ Action	1:18		$115	☐ Revell Collection Club	1:24		$95
☐ Action	1:24		$75	☐ Winner's Circle	1:24		$33
☐ Action	1:64		$18	☐ Winner's Circle Lifetime			
☐ Action/RCCA	1:64		$28	Series	1:64		N/E
☐ Action/RCCA Elite	1:24		$190	☐ Winner's Circle Speedweek	1:64		$12
☐ Revell Collection	1:18		$115	☐			
☐ Revell Collection ▲	1:24		$68	☐			
☐ Revell Collection	1:43		$30	☐			
☐ Revell Collection	1:64		$16				

Note: *Gordon had a solid seven-win season in this car.*

How Many: **Total Value:**   **Notes:**

Page Totals: **How Many**   **Total Value**

COLLECTOR'S **VALUE GUIDE™**

2

DuPont
1999 Chevrolet Monte Carlo

	Scale	LE	Value		Scale	LE	Value
❑ Winner's Circle Gold				❑			
Collection ▲	1:64		$22	❑			
❑				❑			

How Many:	Total Value:	Notes:

3

DuPont – 3-Time Champ
1999 Chevrolet Monte Carlo

	Scale	LE	Value		Scale	LE	Value
❑ Action 24K Gold ▲	1:24		$200	❑			
❑				❑			

How Many:	Total Value:	Notes:

1999

DuPont – Daytona 500
1999 Chevrolet Monte Carlo

	Scale	LE	Value			Scale	LE	Value
❑ Revell Collection	1:24		$80	❑				
❑ Revell Collection	1:64		$19	❑				
❑ Revell Collection Club ▲	1:24		$130	❑				
❑ Winner's Circle	1:64		$13	❑				

How Many:	Total Value:	Notes:

5

DuPont – Fan Club
1999 Chevrolet Monte Carlo

	Scale	LE	Value			Scale	LE	Value
❑ Action/RCCA ▲	1:64		N/E	❑				
❑				❑				

How Many:	Total Value:	Notes:

Page Totals:	How Many	Total Value

COLLECTOR'S
VALUE GUIDE™

NASCAR Racers
1999 Chevrolet Monte Carlo

	Scale	LE	Value		Scale	LE	Value
☐ Action	1:18		$120	☐ Winner's Circle	1:64		N/E
☐ Action ▲	1:24		$110	☐			
☐ Action	1:64		$18	☐			
☐ Action/RCCA	1:64		$30	☐			
☐ Action/RCCA Elite	1:24		$175	☐			

How Many:	Total Value:	Notes:

7

Pepsi
1999 Chevrolet Monte Carlo

	Scale	LE	Value		Scale	LE	Value
☐ Action ▲	1:18		$140	☐ Revell Collection	1:64		$18
☐ Action	1:24		$80	☐ Revell Collection Club	1:18		$145
☐ Action	1:64		$18	☐ Revell Collection Club	1:24		$135
☐ Action/RCCA	1:64		$30	☐ WInner's Circle	1:24		$32
☐ Action/RCCA Elite	1:24		$245	☐ WInner's Circle	1:43		$18
☐ Action/RCCA Elite SelectNet	1:24		N/E	☐ WInner's Circle	1:64		$10
☐ Action/RCCA Elite SelectNet	1:64		N/E	☐			
☐ Revell Collection	1:18		$140	☐			
☐ Revell Collection	1:24		$82	☐			
☐ Revell Collection	1:43		$32				

Note: Gordon drove this Pepsi car in his brief return to Busch Series racing.

How Many:	Total Value:	Notes:

1999

8

Star Wars
1999 Chevrolet Monte Carlo

	Scale	LE	Value		Scale	LE	Value
❑ Action	1:18		$120	❑ Revell Collection	1:64		$18
❑ Action ▲	1:24		$85	❑ Revell Collection Club	1:24		$150
❑ Action	1:64		$18	❑			
❑ Action/RCCA	1:64		$30	❑			
❑ Action/RCCA Elite	1:24		$215	❑			
❑ Revell Collection	1:18		$128	❑			
❑ Revell Collection	1:24		$85				
❑ Revell Collection	1:43		$34				

Note: On May 29, 1999 this car was raced at Charlotte's Lowe's Motor Speedway.

How Many:	Total Value:	Notes:

9

Superman
1999 Chevrolet Monte Carlo

	Scale	LE	Value		Scale	LE	Value
❑ Action	1:18		$135	❑ Revell Collection	1:64		$24
❑ Action ▲	1:24		$100	❑ Revell Collection Club	1:18		$185
❑ Action	1:64		$23	❑ Revell Collection Club	1:24		$175
❑ Action/RCCA	1:32		$66	❑ Winner's Circle Lifetime			
❑ Action/RCCA	1:64		$35	Series	1:64		$10
❑ Action/RCCA Elite	1:24		$250	❑			
❑ Revell Collection	1:24		$100	❑			
❑ Revell Collection	1:43		$40	❑			

How Many:	Total Value:	Notes:

Page Totals:	How Many	Total Value

COLLECTOR'S
VALUE GUIDE™

2000

As NASCAR speeds off into the new millennium, collectors are sure to be enthusiastic about the exciting range of Jeff Gordon die-cast cars to choose from. All the usual suspects turned up in 2000, including the DuPont and Pepsi Chevrolet Monte Carlos. Of special note is the sleek Chevrolet Monte Carlo test car offered by Revell. Another new favorite is the Peanuts paint scheme which celebrates a half century of the beloved Peanuts comic strip. If the past is any indication, collectors of Gordon's die-cast pieces should be in for exciting times ahead!

1

DuPont
2000 Chevrolet Monte Carlo

	Scale	LE	Value		Scale	LE	Value
❑ Action	1:18		$85	❑ Winner's Circle Preview	1:43		$14
❑ Action ▲	1:24		$70	❑ Winner's Circle Preview	1:64		$10
❑ Action	1:64		$15	❑			
❑ Revell Collection	1:64		$16	❑			
❑ Winner's Circle Preview	1:24		$32	❑			

How Many: **Total Value:**   **Notes:**

2000

2

DuPont
2000 Chevrolet Monte Carlo

	Scale	LE	Value		Scale	LE	Value
❑ Action 24K Gold				❑			
(QVC exclusive) ▲	1:24		$185	❑			
❑				❑			

How Many: Total Value: Notes:

3

DuPont – Coca-Cola 600
2000 Chevrolet Monte Carlo

	Scale	LE	Value		Scale	LE	Value
❑ Action	1:18		N/E	❑ Action/RCCA TotalView	1:64		N/E
❑ Action ▲	1:24		N/E	❑ Revell Collection	1:64		N/E
❑ Action	1:64		N/E	❑			
❑ Action/RCCA	1:64		N/E	❑			
❑ Action/RCCA Elite	1:24		N/E	❑			

How Many: Total Value: Notes:

Page Totals:	How Many	Total Value

COLLECTOR'S
VALUE GUIDE™

4

DuPont – Test Car
2000 Chevrolet Monte Carlo

	Scale	LE	Value		Scale	LE	Value
☐ Revell Collection	1:24		$225	☐			
☐				☐			

How Many: | **Total Value:** | **Notes:**

5

NASCAR 2000
2000 Chevrolet Monte Carlo

	Scale	LE	Value		Scale	LE	Value
☐ Action ▲	1:24		$75	☐ Winner's Circle			
☐ Action	1:64		$17	(Kmart exclusive)	1:64		N/E
☐ Action/RCCA	1:64		$28	☐			
☐ Action/RCCA Elite	1:24		$162	☐			
☐ Action/RCCA TotalView	1:64		$30	☐			
☐ Revell Collection Club	1:18		$105	☐			

How Many: | **Total Value:** | **Notes:**

6

Peanuts
2000 Chevrolet Monte Carlo

	Scale	LE	Value		Scale	LE	Value
❑ Action	1:18		N/E	❑ Revell Collection	1:24		N/E
❑ Action ▲	1:24		N/E	❑			
❑ Action	1:64		N/E	❑			
❑ Action/RCCA Elite	1:24		N/E	❑			
❑ Action/RCCA TotalView	1:64		N/E				
❑ Action Total Concept	1:64		N/E				

Note: This car commemorates 50 years of the Peanuts comic strip.

How Many:	Total Value:	Notes:

7

Pepsi
2000 Chevrolet Monte Carlo

	Scale	LE	Value		Scale	LE	Value
❑ Action	1:64		$14	❑			
❑ Action/RCCA Elite ▲	1:24		$120	❑			
❑ Action/RCCA TotalView	1:64		$20	❑			
❑ Revell Collection	1:64		$15	❑			

How Many:	Total Value:	Notes:

Page Totals:	How Many	Total Value

COLLECTOR'S
VALUE GUIDE™

2000

Banks

If you're looking for a place to save your pennies, look no further than these die-cast banks. This section begins with airplane banks, followed alphabetically by car, dually, gas pump, pedal car, pit wagon, Suburban, Tahoe, transporter and truck banks. Make sure you are careful not to spend more than you save!

1

DuPont – 1993 High-Wing

	Scale	LE	Value		Scale	LE	Value
❑ Racing Champions/				❑			
Liberty Classics ▲	1:24		$65	❑			
❑				❑			

How Many:	Total Value:	Notes:

2

DuPont – 1993 Low-Wing

	Scale	LE	Value		Scale	LE	Value
❑ Racing Champions/				❑			
Liberty Classics ▲	1:24		$65	❑			
❑				❑			

How Many:	Total Value:	Notes:

Banks – Airplanes/Cars

3

DuPont – 1993 Rookie Of The Year

	Scale	LE	Value			Scale	LE	Value
❑ Racing Champions/				❑				
Liberty Classics ▲	1:24		$75	❑				
❑				❑				

How Many:	**Total Value:**	**Notes:**

4

DuPont – 1937 Chevrolet Sedan Delivery

	Scale	LE	Value			Scale	LE	Value
❑ Racing Champions ▲	1:25		$300	❑				
❑				❑				

How Many:	**Total Value:**	**Notes:**

5

DuPont – 1955 Chevrolet Convertible

	Scale	LE	Value			Scale	LE	Value
❑ Racing Champions ▲	1:25		$140	❑				
❑				❑				

How Many:	**Total Value:**	**Notes:**

Page Totals:	**How Many**	**Total Value**

COLLECTOR'S
VALUE GUIDE™

6

DuPont – 1955 Chevrolet Sedan Delivery

	Scale	LE	Value		Scale	LE	Value
☐ Racing Champions ▲	1:25		$125	☐			
☐				☐			

How Many: Total Value: Notes:

7

Outback Steakhouse – 1990 Pontiac Grand Prix

	Scale	LE	Value		Scale	LE	Value
☐ Action/RCCA ▲	1:24		N/E	☐			
☐				☐			

How Many: Total Value: Notes:

8

Carolina Ford – 1991 Ford Thunderbird

	Scale	LE	Value		Scale	LE	Value
☐ Action	1:24		$73	☐			
☐ Action/RCCA ▲	1:24		$100	☐			
☐ Action/RCCA Elite				☐			
SelectNet	1:24		$98	☐			

How Many: Total Value: Notes:

Page Totals:	How Many	Total Value

Banks – Cars

9

Baby Ruth – 1992 Ford Thunderbird

	Scale	LE	Value		Scale	LE	Value
❑ Action ▲	1:24		$94	❑			
❑ Action/RCCA	1:24		$135	❑			
❑							

Note: Gordon raced this car in just one – and won $6,285!

How Many: **Total Value:** **Notes:**

10

DuPont – 1993 Chevrolet Lumina

	Scale	LE	Value		Scale	LE	Value
❑ Ertl/White Rose ▲	1:24		$375	❑			
❑				❑			

How Many: **Total Value:** **Notes:**

11

DuPont – 1994 Chevrolet Lumina

	Scale	LE	Value		Scale	LE	Value
❑ Racing Champions ▲	1:24		$160	❑			
❑							
❑							

Note: Gordon was the first driver to win a Winston Cup race in a car with the number 24.

How Many: **Total Value:** **Notes:**

Page Totals:	How Many	Total Value

COLLECTOR'S
VALUE GUIDE™

12

DuPont / Brickyard Winner – 1994 Chevrolet Lumina

	Scale	LE	Value			Scale	LE	Value
☐ Racing Champions ▲	1:24		$220	☐				
☐				☐				

How Many: | **Total Value:** | **Notes:**

13

PHOTO
UNAVAILABLE

DuPont / Coca-Cola 600 Winner – 1994 Chevrolet Monte Carlo

	Scale	LE	Value			Scale	LE	Value
☐ Racing Champions ▲	1:24		$365	☐				
☐				☐				

How Many: | **Total Value:**

14

DuPont – 1995 Chevrolet Monte Carlo

	Scale	LE	Value			Scale	LE	Value
☐ Action ▲	1:24		$170	☐				
☐ Racing Champions	1:24		$95	☐				
☐				☐				

How Many: | **Total Value:** | **Notes:**

COLLECTOR'S
VALUE GUIDE™

Page Totals:	How Many	Total Value

Banks – Cars

15

DuPont / Winston Cup Champion – 1995 Chevrolet Monte Carlo

	Scale	LE	Value		Scale	LE	Value
❑ Action ▲	1:24		$200	❑			
❑ Racing Champions				❑			
Signature Series	1:24		$135	❑			

How Many: **Total Value:**   **Notes:**

16

DuPont – 1996 Chevrolet Monte Carlo

	Scale	LE	Value		Scale	LE	Value
❑ Action ▲	1:24		$105	❑			
❑				❑			

How Many: **Total Value:**   **Notes:**

17

DuPont – 1996 Chevrolet Monte Carlo

	Scale	LE	Value		Scale	LE	Value
❑ Racing Champions				❑			
Chrome Chase ▲	1:24		$1,075	❑			
❑				❑			

How Many: **Total Value:**   **Notes:**

Page Totals:	**How Many**	**Total Value**

COLLECTOR'S
VALUE GUIDE™

18

Chroma Premier – 1997 Chevrolet Monte Carlo

	Scale	LE	Value		Scale	LE	Value
❑ Action ▲	1:24		$225	❑			
❑				❑			

How Many: **Total Value:** **Notes:**

19

PHOTO
UNAVAILABLE

DuPont – 1997 Chevrolet Monte Carlo

	Scale	LE	Value		Scale	LE	Value
❑ Action/RCCA	1:24		$135	❑			
❑				❑			

How Many: **Total Value:** **Notes:**

20

Jurassic Park – 1997 Chevrolet Monte Carlo

	Scale	LE	Value		Scale	LE	Value
❑ Action ▲	1:24		$200	❑			
❑				❑			

How Many: **Total Value:** **Notes:**

COLLECTOR'S
VALUE GUIDE™

Page Totals:	How Many	Total Value

Banks – Cars

21

Million Dollar Date – 1997 Chevrolet Monte Carlo

	Scale	LE	Value		Scale	LE	Value
☐ Action ▲	1:24		$160	☐			
☐ Action (Mac Tools sleeve)	1:24		$165	☐			
☐				☐			

How Many: **Total Value:**   **Notes:**

22

ChromaLusion – 1998 Chevrolet Monte Carlo

	Scale	LE	Value		Scale	LE	Value
☐ Action ▲	1:24		$160	☐			
☐ Action/RCCA	1:24		$185	☐			
☐				☐			

How Many: **Total Value:**   **Notes:**

23

DuPont – 1998 Chevrolet Monte Carlo

	Scale	LE	Value		Scale	LE	Value
☐ Action ▲	1:24		$75	☐			
☐ Action/RCCA	1:24		$98	☐			
☐				☐			

How Many: **Total Value:**   **Notes:**

Page Totals:	**How Many**	**Total Value**

COLLECTOR'S VALUE GUIDE™

24

DuPont / No Bull – 1998 Chevrolet Monte Carlo

	Scale	LE	Value		Scale	LE	Value
❏ Action	1:24		$90	❏			
❏ Action/RCCA ▲	1:24		$105	❏			
❏				❏			

How Many: **Total Value:**   **Notes:**

25

DuPont – 1999 Chevrolet Monte Carlo

	Scale	LE	Value		Scale	LE	Value
❏ Action	1:24		$70	❏			
❏ Action/RCCA ▲	1:24		$88	❏			
❏							
❏							

Note: 1999 was the year of the sevens for Gordon: seven victories, seven did-not-finishes and seven poles.

How Many: **Total Value:**   **Notes:**

26

NASCAR Racers – 1999 Chevrolet Monte Carlo

	Scale	LE	Value		Scale	LE	Value
❏ Action/RCCA ▲	1:24		$90	❏			
❏				❏			

How Many: **Total Value:**   **Notes:**

	How Many	**Total Value**
Page Totals:		

Banks – Cars

27

Pepsi – 1999 Chevrolet Monte Carlo

	Scale	LE	Value			Scale	LE	Value
❑ Action	1:24		$87	❑				
❑ Action/RCCA ▲	1:24		$108	❑				
❑ Action/RCCA Elite				❑				
SelectNet	1:24		$95	❑				

How Many: **Total Value:**   **Notes:**

28

Star Wars – 1999 Chevrolet Monte Carlo

	Scale	LE	Value			Scale	LE	Value
❑ Action ▲	1:24		$74	❑				
❑ Action/RCCA	1:24		$95	❑				
❑				❑				

How Many: **Total Value:**   **Notes:**

29

Superman – 1999 Chevrolet Monte Carlo

	Scale	LE	Value			Scale	LE	Value
❑ Action	1:24		$90	❑				
❑ Action/RCCA ▲	1:24		$110	❑				
❑				❑				

How Many: **Total Value:**   **Notes:**

Page Totals:	How Many	Total Value

COLLECTOR'S VALUE GUIDE™

30

DuPont – 2000 Chevrolet Monte Carlo

	Scale	LE	Value		Scale	LE	Value
☐ Action	1:24		$70	☐			
☐ Action/RCCA ▲	1:24		$80	☐			
☐				☐			

How Many: Total Value: Notes:

31

NASCAR 2000 – 2000 Chevrolet Monte Carlo

	Scale	LE	Value		Scale	LE	Value
☐ Action	1:24		$75	☐			
☐ Action/RCCA ▲	1:24		$90	☐			
☐				☐			

How Many: Total Value: Notes:

32

DuPont – 1994 Dually

	Scale	LE	Value		Scale	LE	Value
☐ Action ▲	1:24		$145	☐			
☐				☐			

How Many: Total Value: Notes:

COLLECTOR'S **VALUE GUIDE**™

Page Totals:	How Many	Total Value

Banks – Cars/Duallies

Banks – Duallies/Gas Pumps

33

DuPont – 1995 Dually

	Scale	LE	Value			Scale	LE	Value
❑ Action ▲	1:24		$145		❑			
❑					❑			

How Many: **Total Value:**   **Notes:**

34

Jurassic Park – 1997 Gas Pump

	Scale	LE	Value			Scale	LE	Value
❑ Action ▲	1:16		N/E		❑			
❑					❑			

How Many: **Total Value:**   **Notes:**

35

ChromaLusion – 1998 Gas Pump

	Scale	LE	Value			Scale	LE	Value
❑ Action ▲	1:16		$65		❑			
❑					❑			

How Many: **Total Value:**   **Notes:**

Page Totals:	How Many	Total Value

COLLECTOR'S **VALUE GUIDE**™

36

DuPont – 1999 Gas Pump

	Scale	LE	Value		Scale	LE	Value
❏ Action ▲	1:16		$45	❏			
❏				❏			

How Many: **Total Value:**   **Notes:**

37

Pepsi – 1999 Gas Pump

	Scale	LE	Value		Scale	LE	Value
❏ Action ▲	1:16		$48	❏			
❏				❏			

How Many: **Total Value:**   **Notes:**

38

Superman – 1999 Gas Pump

	Scale	LE	Value		Scale	LE	Value
❏ Action ▲	1:16		$53	❏			
❏				❏			

How Many: **Total Value:**   **Notes:**

COLLECTOR'S
VALUE GUIDE™

Page Totals:	How Many	Total Value

Banks – Gas Pumps/Pedal Cars

39

NASCAR 2000 – 2000 Gas Pump

	Scale	LE	Value			Scale	LE	Value
☐ Action ▲	1:16		N/E	☐				
☐				☐				

How Many:	Total Value:		Notes:	

40

DuPont – 1999 Pedal Car

	Scale	LE	Value			Scale	LE	Value
☐ Action ▲	1:43		$38	☐				
☐				☐				

How Many:	Total Value:		Notes:	

41

Star Wars – 1999 Pedal Car

	Scale	LE	Value			Scale	LE	Value
☐ Action ▲	1:43		N/E	☐				
☐				☐				

How Many:	Total Value:		Notes:	

Page Totals:	How Many	Total Value

COLLECTOR'S **VALUE GUIDE™**

42

Superman – 1999 Pedal Car

	Scale	LE	Value		Scale	LE	Value
☐ Action ▲	1:43		N/E	☐			
☐				☐			

How Many: Total Value: Notes:

43

DuPont / Rookie Of The Year – 1993 Pit Wagon

	Scale	LE	Value		Scale	LE	Value
☐ Action ▲	1:16		N/E	☐			
☐				☐			

How Many: Total Value: Notes:

44

DuPont – 1994 Pit Wagon

	Scale	LE	Value		Scale	LE	Value
☐ Action/RCCA ▲	1:16		$115	☐			
☐				☐			

How Many: Total Value: Notes:

COLLECTOR'S VALUE GUIDE™

Page Totals: How Many   Total Value

45

Jurassic Park – 1997 Pit Wagon

	Scale	LE	Value			Scale	LE	Value
☐ Action ▲	1:16		$54		☐			
☐					☐			

How Many:	Total Value:	Notes:

46

Pepsi – 1999 Pit Wagon

	Scale	LE	Value			Scale	LE	Value
☐ Action ▲	1:16		$60		☐			
☐					☐			

How Many:	Total Value:	Notes:

47

Superman – 1999 Pit Wagon

	Scale	LE	Value			Scale	LE	Value
☐ Action ▲	1:16		$56		☐			
☐					☐			

How Many:	Total Value:	Notes:

Page Totals:	How Many	Total Value

COLLECTOR'S
VALUE GUIDE™

48

DuPont – 1993 Chevrolet Suburban

	Scale	LE	Value			Scale	LE	Value
❑ Brookfield Collector's				❑				
Guild ▲	1:25		N/E	❑				
❑				❑				

How Many: **Total Value:** **Notes:**

49

DuPont – 1997 Chevrolet Suburban

	Scale	LE	Value			Scale	LE	Value
❑ Brookfield Collector's				❑				
Guild ▲	1:25		N/E	❑				
❑				❑				

How Many: **Total Value:** **Notes:**

50

DuPont – 1996 Chevrolet Tahoe

	Scale	LE	Value			Scale	LE	Value
❑ Brookfield Collector's				❑				
Guild ▲	1:25		N/E	❑				
❑				❑				

How Many: **Total Value:** **Notes:**

COLLECTOR'S VALUE GUIDE™

Page Totals:	**How Many**	**Total Value**

Banks – Transporters/Delivery Trucks

51

DuPont – 1995 Transporter

	Scale	LE	Value		Scale	LE	Value
❑ Racing Champions				❑			
Premier ▲	1:64		$50	❑			
❑				❑			

How Many:	Total Value:	Notes:

52

PHOTO UNAVAILABLE

Baby Ruth – 1932 Ford Panel Delivery Truck

	Scale	LE	Value		Scale	LE	Value
❑ Ertl	1:25		$350	❑			
❑				❑			

How Many:	Total Value:	Notes:

Page Totals:	How Many	Total Value

Commemorative Cars

Although Gordon never drove any of these vehicles around a racetrack, they are a fun and unique addition to any collection. The Winner's Circle Cool Custom line and the die-cast manufacturer Brookfield Collector's Guild have both released some pretty snazzy die-cast replicas of some pretty classic cars.

1

DuPont – 1957 Chevrolet Bel Aire

	Scale	LE	Value		Scale	LE	Value
❑ Winner's Circle				❑			
Cool Custom	1:64		$12	❑			
❑				❑			

How Many:	Total Value:	Notes:

2

Pepsi – 1957 Chevrolet Bel Aire

	Scale	LE	Value		Scale	LE	Value
❑ Winner's Circle				❑			
Cool Custom ▲	1:64		$12	❑			
❑				❑			

How Many:	Total Value:	Notes:

Page Totals:	How Many	Total Value

Commemorative Cars

3

DuPont – 1957 Chevrolet Bel Aire Convertible

	Scale	LE	Value			Scale	LE	Value
☐ Winner's Circle					☐			
Cool Custom ▲	1:64		$12		☐			
☐					☐			

How Many: **Total Value:** **Notes:**

4

PHOTO
UNAVAILABLE

DuPont – 1958 Chevrolet Corvette

	Scale	LE	Value			Scale	LE	Value
☐ Winner's Circle					☐			
Cool Custom	1:64		$12		☐			
☐					☐			

How Many: **Total Value:** **Notes:**

5

DuPont – 1963 Chevrolet Impala

	Scale	LE	Value			Scale	LE	Value
☐ Winner's Circle					☐			
Cool Custom ▲	1:64		$12		☐			
☐					☐			

How Many: **Total Value:** **Notes:**

Page Totals:	How Many	Total Value

COLLECTOR'S
VALUE GUIDE™

6

DuPont – 1998 Chevrolet Corvette

	Scale	LE	Value		Scale	LE	Value
❑ Brookfield Collector's				❑			
Guild ▲	1:25		N/E	❑			
❑				❑			

How Many:	Total Value:	Notes:

Crystal Cars

Collectors searching for something new and different to add to their collections don't have to look any farther than Action/RCCA's Crystal Series. Since Action began producing these exquisite crystal cars in 1999, the company has released four Jeff Gordon reproductions, including his 1992 Baby Ruth car and his 1999 Superman paint scheme.

1

Baby Ruth – 1992 Ford Thunderbird

	Scale	LE	Value		Scale	LE	Value
❑ Action/RCCA Crystal ▲	1:24		N/E	❑			
❑				❑			

How Many:	Total Value:	Notes:

Page Totals:	How Many	Total Value

2

DuPont – 1999 Chevrolet Monte Carlo

	Scale	LE	Value		Scale	LE	Value
☐ Action/RCCA Crystal ▲	1:24		$80	☐			
☐				☐			

How Many: **Total Value:** **Notes:**

3

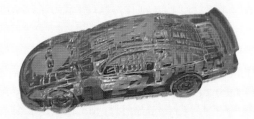

Pepsi – 1999 Chevrolet Monte Carlo

	Scale	LE	Value		Scale	LE	Value
☐ Action/RCCA Crystal ▲	1:24		$72	☐			
☐				☐			

How Many: **Total Value:** **Notes:**

4

PHOTO
UNAVAILABLE

Superman – 1999 Chevrolet Monte Carlo

	Scale	LE	Value		Scale	LE	Value
☐ Action/RCCA Crystal	1:24		$95	☐			
☐				☐			

How Many: **Total Value:** **Notes:**

Page Totals:	How Many	Total Value

COLLECTOR'S
VALUE GUIDE™

Duallies

Duallies are a hot collectible item and there are several options for collecting them. They come either without attached trailers, with attached trailers or as part of a set with a trailer and car. Duallies and their accessories are not limited to the standard Gordon rainbow paint scheme, which should come as very pleasing news to collectors.

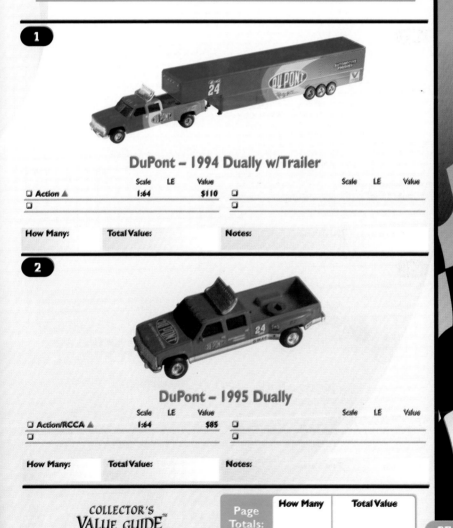

1

DuPont – 1994 Dually w/Trailer

	Scale	LE	Value		Scale	LE	Value
☐ Action ▲	1:64		$110	☐			
☐				☐			

How Many: Total Value: Notes:

2

DuPont – 1995 Dually

	Scale	LE	Value		Scale	LE	Value
☐ Action/RCCA ▲	1:64		$85	☐			
☐				☐			

How Many: Total Value: Notes:

Page Totals:	How Many	Total Value

3

DuPont – 1996 Dually

	Scale	LE	Value		Scale	LE	Value
❑ Action	1:64		$25	❑			
❑				❑			

How Many: **Total Value:**   **Notes:**

4

DuPont – 1996 Dually w/Trailer & Car

	Scale	LE	Value		Scale	LE	Value
❑ Brookfield Collector's Guild	1:25		N/E	❑			
❑				❑			
				❑			

How Many: **Total Value:**   **Notes:**

5

Jurassic Park – 1997 Dually w/Trailer

	Scale	LE	Value		Scale	LE	Value
❑ Brookfield Collector's Guild ▲	1:25		N/E	❑			
❑				❑			

How Many: **Total Value:**   **Notes:**

Page Totals:	How Many	Total Value

COLLECTOR'S
VALUE GUIDE™

6

ChromaLusion – 1998 Dually w/Trailer

	Scale	LE	Value		Scale	LE	Value
☐ Action ▲	1:64		$100	☐			
☐ Brookfield Collector's				☐			
Guild	1:25		$122	☐			

How Many: **Total Value:** **Notes:**

7

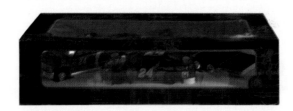

ChromaLusion – 1998 Dually w/Trailer & Car

	Scale	LE	Value		Scale	LE	Value
☐ Brookfield Collector's				☐			
Guild ▲	1:25		$110	☐			
☐				☐			

How Many: **Total Value:** **Notes:**

8

PHOTO
UNAVAILABLE

DuPont – 1998 Dually

	Scale	LE	Value		Scale	LE	Value
☐ Action	1:25		$90	☐			
☐				☐			

How Many: **Total Value:** **Notes:**

COLLECTOR'S
VALUE GUIDE™

Page Totals:	How Many	Total Value

Duallies

9

DuPont – 1998 Dually w/Trailer

	Scale	LE	Value		Scale	LE	Value
☐ Action ▲	1:64		$80	☐			
☐				☐			

How Many: | **Total Value:** | **Notes:**

10

DuPont – 1999 Dually w/Trailer & Car

	Scale	LE	Value		Scale	LE	Value
☐ Brookfield Collector's Guild ▲	1:25		$110	☐			
☐				☐			
				☐			

How Many: | **Total Value:** | **Notes:**

11

Superman – 1999 Dually w/Trailer & Car

	Scale	LE	Value		Scale	LE	Value
☐ Brookfield Collector's Guild ▲	1:25		$150	☐			
☐				☐			
				☐			

How Many: | **Total Value:** | **Notes:**

Page Totals:	How Many	Total Value

COLLECTOR'S VALUE GUIDE™

Helmets

Collectible helmets have been increasing in popularity among collectors of racing memorabilia. Noted racing collectibles manufacturer Action produces a line of 1:4 scale helmets for regular-distribution, and a line of 1:3 scale helmets for club distribution. The Peanuts helmet is an exception to this, as it comes in a 1:2 scale.

1

DuPont – 1997 Helmet

	Scale	LE	Value		Scale	LE	Value
☐ Simpson ▲	1:4		N/E	☐			
☐				☐			

How Many: **Total Value:** **Notes:**

2

ChromaLusion – 1998 Helmet

	Scale	LE	Value		Scale	LE	Value
☐ Action ▲	1:4		$55	☐			
☐				☐			

How Many: **Total Value:** **Notes:**

Page Totals:	How Many	Total Value

Helmets

3

Pepsi – 1999 Helmet

	Scale	LE	Value		Scale	LE	Value
☐ Action	1:4		$40	☐			
☐ Action/RCCA ▲	1:3		$50	☐			
☐				☐			

How Many: **Total Value:** **Notes:**

4

Superman – 1999 Helmet

	Scale	LE	Value		Scale	LE	Value
☐ Action	1:4		$28	☐			
☐ Action/RCCA ▲	1:3		$55	☐			
☐				☐			

How Many: **Total Value:** **Notes:**

5

PHOTO
UNAVAILABLE

Peanuts – 2000 Helmet

	Scale	LE	Value		Scale	LE	Value
☐ Action	1:2		N/E	☐			
☐				☐			

How Many: **Total Value:** **Notes:**

Page Totals:	How Many	Total Value

COLLECTOR'S
VALUE GUIDE™

Pit Scenes

The pit crew is an integral part of NASCAR racing. It is therefore fitting that several manufacturers, including Racing Champions and Winner's Circle, have produced collectible sets featuring Jeff Gordon's pit crew, the Rainbow Warriors.

1

DuPont – 1995 Pit Stop Crew

	Scale	LE	Value		Scale	LE	Value
❑ Racing Champions ▲	1:24		N/E	❑			
❑				❑			

How Many: **Total Value:**   **Notes:**

2

DuPont – 1998 Four Tire Stop

	Scale	LE	Value		Scale	LE	Value
❑ Winner's Circle Pit Row ▲	1:64		$20	❑			
❑				❑			

How Many: **Total Value:**   **Notes:**

Page Totals:	How Many	Total Value

3

DuPont – 1998 Moving Into Position

	Scale	LE	Value		Scale	LE	Value
❑ Winner's Circle Pit Row ▲	1:64		$20	❑			
❑				❑			

How Many: Total Value: Notes:

4

DuPont – 1998 Two Tire Stop

	Scale	LE	Value		Scale	LE	Value
❑ Winner's Circle Pit Row ▲	1:64		$20	❑			
❑				❑			

How Many: Total Value: Notes:

5

**PHOTO
UNAVAILABLE**

Million Dollar Win – 1999 Tires Off

	Scale	LE	Value		Scale	LE	Value
❑ Winner's Circle Pit Row	1:64		$20	❑			
❑				❑			

How Many: Total Value: Notes:

Page Totals:	How Many	Total Value

COLLECTOR'S
VALUE GUIDE™

6

Pepsi – 1999 Coming In

	Scale	LE	Value		Scale	LE	Value
❑ Winner's Circle Pit Row ▲	1:64		$25	❑			
❑				❑			

How Many: **Total Value:**   **Notes:**

7

Star Wars – 1999 Tires On

	Scale	LE	Value		Scale	LE	Value
❑ Winner's Circle Pit Row ▲	1:64		N/E	❑			
❑				❑			

How Many: **Total Value:**   **Notes:**

8

Superman – 1999 Pit Crew

	Scale	LE	Value		Scale	LE	Value
❑ Winner's Circle Pit Row ▲	1:64		N/E	❑			
❑				❑			

How Many: **Total Value:**   **Notes:**

COLLECTOR'S VALUE GUIDE™

Page Totals:	How Many	Total Value

Pit Scenes

Sets

Sets include everything from promotional products that team Gordon's car with the car of another driver to three-vehicle "fantasy packs" that include a car, boat and airplane. There are even two train sets included in this section. With this much variety, you're sure to find something that will get your motor revving!

1

PHOTO UNAVAILABLE

Carolina Ford – 1991 Gordon/Martin (set/2)

	Scale	LE	Value			Scale	LE	Value
❑ Racing Champions	1:64		$50		❑			
❑					❑			

How Many: **Total Value:**   **Notes:**

2

DuPont – 1993 Racing Team (set/2)

	Scale	LE	Value			Scale	LE	Value
❑ Matchbox Superstars					❑			
Team Convoy ▲	1:64		$150		❑			
❑					❑			

How Many: **Total Value:**   **Notes:**

Page Totals:	How Many	Total Value

3

DuPont – 1994 Brickyard 400 (set/2)

	Scale	LE	Value			Scale	LE	Value
❏ Brookfield Collector's Guild ▲	1:25		$105	❏				
❏				❏				
				❏				

How Many:	Total Value:	Notes:

4

Kellogg's Frosted Mini-Wheats Collector Set – 1994 (set/3)

	Scale	LE	Value			Scale	LE	Value
❏ Racing Champions ▲	1:64		$70	❏				
❏				❏				

How Many:	Total Value:	Notes:

5

PHOTO
UNAVAILABLE

Brickyard Special – 1995 Gordon/Earnhardt

	Scale	LE	Value			Scale	LE	Value
❏ Action	1:64		$44	❏				
❏				❏				

How Many:	Total Value:	Notes:

COLLECTOR'S
VALUE GUIDE™

Page Totals:	How Many	Total Value

Sets

Sets

6

DuPont – 1995 Car w/Super Truck

	Scale	LE	Value			Scale	LE	Value
❑ Racing Champions				❑				
Signature Series ▲	1:64		$23	❑				
❑				❑				

How Many: **Total Value:**   **Notes:**

7

Kellogg's Mini-Wheats Special – 1995 Gordon/Earnhardt (set/2)

	Scale	LE	Value			Scale	LE	Value
❑ Action ▲	1:64		$42	❑				
❑				❑				
❑								

Note: These cars come packaged in a box that looks just like a box of Kellogg's Frosted Mini-Wheats.

How Many: **Total Value:**   **Notes:**

8

PHOTO UNAVAILABLE

DuPont – 1996 Train Set w/Car

	Scale	LE	Value			Scale	LE	Value
❑ Revell	1:64		$100	❑				
❑				❑				

How Many: **Total Value:**   **Notes:**

Page Totals:	**How Many**	**Total Value**

COLLECTOR'S **VALUE GUIDE**™

9

Jurassic Park – 1997 Train Set w/Cars

	Scale	LE	Value		Scale	LE	Value
❑ Revell ▲	1:64		$80	❑			
❑				❑			

How Many: **Total Value:**   **Notes:**

10

Kellogg's Mini-Wheats Promo – 1997 (set/3)

	Scale	LE	Value		Scale	LE	Value
❑ Action ▲	1:64		N/E	❑			
❑				❑			

How Many: **Total Value:**   **Notes:**

11

DuPont – 1998 (set/3)

	Scale	LE	Value		Scale	LE	Value
❑ Winner's Circle Fantasy Pack ▲	1:64		$16	❑			
❑				❑			

How Many: **Total Value:**   **Notes:**

Sets

Sets

12

DuPont – 1998 (set/3, w/Gold Car)

	Scale	LE	Value		Scale	LE	Value
❑ Brookfield Collector's				❑			
Guild ▲	1:25		$185	❑			
❑				❑			

How Many:	Total Value:	Notes:

13

DuPont – 1999 (set/3)

	Scale	LE	Value		Scale	LE	Value
❑ Winner's Circle				❑			
Fantasy Pack ▲	1:64		N/E	❑			
❑				❑			

How Many:	Total Value:	Notes:

14

DuPont – 1999 Car w/Hood

	Scale	LE	Value		Scale	LE	Value
❑ Winner's Circle Deluxe ▲	1:64		$11	❑			
❑				❑			

How Many:	Total Value:	Notes:

Page Totals:	How Many	Total Value

COLLECTOR'S VALUE GUIDE™

15

PHOTO
UNAVAILABLE

DuPont – 1999 Support Vehicle Set

	Scale	LE	Value		Scale	LE	Value
☐ Winner's Circle Track				☐			
Support Crew	1:64		$18	☐			
☐				☐			

How Many: **Total Value:**   **Notes:**

16

Pepsi – 1999 (set/3)

	Scale	LE	Value		Scale	LE	Value
☐ Winner's Circle				☐			
Fantasy Pack ▲	1:64		$16	☐			
☐				☐			

How Many: **Total Value:**   **Notes:**

17

Pepsi – 1999 Car w/Helmet

	Scale	LE	Value		Scale	LE	Value
☐ Action ▲	1:32		$66	☐			
☐				☐			

How Many: **Total Value:**   **Notes:**

Page Totals:	How Many	Total Value

Sets

Sets

18

Pepsi – 1999 Support Vehicle Set

	Scale	LE	Value		Scale	LE	Value
❑ Winner's Circle Track				❑			
Support Crew ▲	1:64		$18	❑			
❑				❑			

How Many: **Total Value:**   **Notes:**

19

Superman – 1999 (set/9)

	Scale	LE	Value		Scale	LE	Value
❑ Action ▲	1:64		N/E	❑			
❑				❑			

How Many: **Total Value:**   **Notes:**

20

Superman – 1999 (set/3)

	Scale	LE	Value		Scale	LE	Value
❑ Winner's Circle				❑			
Fantasy Pack ▲	1:64		$16	❑			
❑				❑			

How Many: **Total Value:**   **Notes:**

Page Totals:	How Many	Total Value

Suburbans

Brookfield Collector's Guild's attractive die-cast Suburbans should prove especially enticing to collectors who want to build a complete set in the Superman or Pepsi paint scheme. The Pepsi Suburban even comes with an attached flatbed trailer and die-cast reproduction of Gordon's Pepsi car.

1

Pepsi – 1999 Suburban w/Car

	Scale	LE	Value		Scale	LE	Value
☐ Brookfield Collector's				☐			
Guild ▲	1:25		N/E	☐			
☐				☐			

How Many: | **Total Value:** | **Notes:**

2

Superman – 1999 Suburban

	Scale	LE	Value		Scale	LE	Value
☐ Brookfield Collector's				☐			
Guild ▲	1:25		$115	☐			
☐				☐			

How Many: | **Total Value:** | **Notes:**

Transporters

These big rig beauties are the backbone of every race team – after all, if it weren't for their transporters, how would the drivers get their cars from race to race? Transporters have been produced by almost every die-cast manufacturer, and trace Jeff Gordon's career from his earliest racing days all the way to the new millennium.

1

Baby Ruth – 1992 Transporter

	Scale	LE	Value		Scale	LE	Value
❑ Action/Peachstate	1:64		$230	❑			
❑ Matchbox/White Rose				❑			
Super Stars ▲	1:64		$175	❑			
❑ Racing Champions	1:64		$120	❑			

How Many: **Total Value:**   **Notes:**

2

DuPont – 1993 Transporter

	Scale	LE	Value		Scale	LE	Value
❑ Matchbox/White Rose				❑ Racing Champions Premier	1:87		$64
Super Stars	1:87		$37	❑ Winross	1:64		$105
❑ Racing Champions	1:43		$120	❑			
❑ Racing Champions ▲	1:64		$58	❑			
❑ Racing Champions	1:87		$22	❑			
❑ Racing Champions Premier	1:64		$80	❑			

Page Totals:	How Many	Total Value

COLLECTOR'S
VALUE GUIDE™

3

DuPont – 1994 Transporter

	Scale	LE	Value		Scale	LE	Value
❑ Action	1:64		$115	❑ Racing Champions	1:87		$30
❑ Racing Champions	1:43		$88	❑			
❑ Racing Champions ▲	1:64		$56	❑			

How Many: **Total Value:** **Notes:**

4

DuPont – 1995 Transporter

	Scale	LE	Value		Scale	LE	Value
❑ Action	1:96		$68	❑ Racing Champions Premier	1:87		$50
❑ Nylint Steel	1:25		$118	❑ Racing Champions			
❑ Race Image by				Signature Series	1:64		$48
Corgi Haulers	1:64		$45	❑			
❑ Racing Champions ▲	1:64		$50	❑			
❑ Racing Champions Premier	1:64		$82	❑			

How Many: **Total Value:** **Notes:**

5

DuPont – 1996 Transporter

	Scale	LE	Value		Scale	LE	Value
❑ Matchbox/White Rose				❑			
Super Stars	1:80		$18	❑			
❑ Racing Champions ▲	1:64		$45	❑			
❑ Racing Champions Premier	1:87		$50	❑			

How Many: **Total Value:** **Notes:**

Page Totals:	**How Many**	**Total Value**

Transporters

Transporters

6

DuPont – 1997 Transporter

	Scale	LE	Value			Scale	LE	Value
☐ Racing Champions ▲	1:64		$35	☐				
☐ Racing Champions	1:87		N/E	☐				
☐ Racing Champions	1:144		$20	☐				
☐ Racing Champions Preview	1:64		$30	☐				

How Many: **Total Value:**   **Notes:**

7

DuPont – 1998 Transporter w/Car

	Scale	LE	Value			Scale	LE	Value
☐ Revell Select ▲	1:64		$52	☐				
☐				☐				

How Many: **Total Value:**   **Notes:**

8

DuPont – 2000 Transporter

	Scale	LE	Value			Scale	LE	Value
☐ Winner's Circle ▲	1:64		$18	☐				
☐				☐				

How Many: **Total Value:**   **Notes:**

Page Totals:	**How Many**	**Total Value**

COLLECTOR'S
VALUE GUIDE™

Trading Cards

A list of all the trading cards with Jeff Gordon images follows on the next several pages. They are listed alphabetically by manufacturer, and appear in chronological order, the oldest cars first. The list then proceeds alphabetically.

Action Packed

1993

		Value
❑ 1993	#32	$9.00
❑ 1993	#86	$5.00
❑ 1993	#87	$2.00
❑ 1993	#93	$4.25
❑ 1993	#173	$3.25
❑ 1993	#205	$2.25
❑ 1993	#156	$3.75
❑ 1993	24KT Gold #55G	$70.00
❑ 1993	Promo #JG1	$42.00
❑ 1993	Young Guns #61	$6.00
❑ 1993	Young Guns #150	$4.00
❑ 1993	Young Guns #153	$4.00
❑ 1993	Young Guns 24KT Gold #10G	$100.00
❑ 1993	Young Guns 24KT Gold #12G	$100.00
❑ 1993	Young Guns 24KT Gold #26G	$75.00
❑ 1993	Young Guns 24KT Gold #29G	$75.00

1994

		Value
❑ 1994	#14	$3.50
❑ 1994	#73	$3.50
❑ 1994	#146	$3.50

Action Packed, cont.

		Value
❑ 1994	#209	$3.00
❑ 1994	24KT Gold #27G	$85.00
❑ 1994	24KT Gold #189G	$320.00
❑ 1994	Daytona Review #103	$3.00
❑ 1994	Promo #2R942	$14.00
❑ 1994	Promo #2R942G	$180.00
❑ 1994	Promo #3R94S	$13.00
❑ 1994	Winston Cup Rookie Of The Year #30	$3.50

1995

❑ 1995	Promo #102	N/E
❑ 1995	Promo Team Rainbow	$9.00
❑ 1995	Winston Cup Country #63	$2.00
❑ 1995	Winston Cup Country 24KT Gold #1	$50.00
❑ 1995	Winston Cup Country 24KT Gold #2	$50.00
❑ 1995	Winston Cup Country 24KT Gold #3	$50.00
❑ 1995	Winston Cup Preview #9	$2.00
❑ 1995	Winston Cup Preview 24KT Gold #2G	$75.00
❑ 1995	Winston Cup Stars 24KT Gold #2G	$60.00
❑ 1995	Winston Cup Stars 24KT Gold #4G	$60.00
❑ 1995	Winston Cup Stars 24KT Gold #6G	$60.00
❑ 1995	Winston Cup Stars 24KT Gold #19G	$60.00
❑ 1995	Winston Cup Stars 24KT Gold #20G	$60.00
❑ 1995	Winston Cup Stars Out Of The Chute #24	$2.00
❑ 1995	Winston Cup Stars Race Winners #47	$2.00
❑ 1995	Winston Cup Stars Race Winners #49	$2.00
❑ 1995	Winston Cup Stars Race Winners #51	$2.00

1996

❑ 1996	Credentials #20	$2.25
❑ 1996	Credentials Checklist #105	$1.25
❑ 1996	Credentials FanScan #4	$60.00
❑ 1996	Credentials Leaders Of The Pack #5	$20.00

Page Totals:	How Many	Total Value

Trading Cards

Action Packed, cont.		Value
❑ 1996	Credentials Leaders Of The Pack #8	$20.00
❑ 1996	Credentials Oversized #2	$7.00
❑ 1996	Promo Leader Pack #5	N/E

Card Dynamics

1993-95

| ❑ 1993-95 | Double Eagle Post Cards Metallic Baby Ruth | $125.00 |
| ❑ 1993-95 | Double Eagle Post Cards Metallic DuPont | $120.00 |

1993

| ❑ 1993 | Gant Oil Metallic | $18.00 |

1994

| ❑ 1994 | Blacktop Busch Series Metallic | $14.00 |
| ❑ 1994 | Gant Oil Metallic | $13.00 |

Classic

1995

❑ 1995	Assets #3	$2.00
❑ 1995	Assets #31	$2.00
❑ 1995	Assets Gold Signature Cards #3	N/E
❑ 1995	Assets Gold Signature Cards #31	N/E
❑ 1995	Images #24	$2.00
❑ 1995	Images #72	$2.50
❑ 1995	Images #100	N/E
❑ 1995	Images Driven Red Box #D2	$9.00
❑ 1995	Images Hard Chargers Black Box #HC8	$7.00

Number 24 races to the finish line on this Upper Deck Collector's Choice card!

Classic, cont.		Value
❑ 1995	Images Owner's Pride #OP5	$7.00
❑ 1995	Scoreboard Promo Images	$17.00

1996

❑ 1996	Assets #2	$2.00
❑ 1996	Autographed Racing #2	$2.25
❑ 1996	Autographed Racing Autographs #16	$190.00

Finish Line

1993

❑ 1993	#83	$2.00
❑ 1993	#110	$2.00
❑ 1993	Promo #P2	N/E
❑ 1993	Silver #83	$6.00
❑ 1993	Silver #110	$6.00

1994

❑ 1994	#36	$2.00
❑ 1994	#75	$2.00
❑ 1994	Gold #11	$2.00
❑ 1994	Gold #28	$2.00
❑ 1994	Gold #60	$2.00
❑ 1994	Gold #88	$2.00
❑ 1994	Promo Gold #P1	$7.00
❑ 1994	Rookie of the Year NNO	$5.50
❑ 1994	Silver #75	$5.00

1995

❑ 1995	#24	$2.00
❑ 1995	#53	$2.00
❑ 1995	#67	$1.50
❑ 1995	#105	$2.00
❑ 1995	Gold Signatures #GS1	$55.00
❑ 1995	Printer's Proof #24	$60.00
❑ 1995	Printer's Proof #105	$60.00
❑ 1995	Standout Drivers #SD7	$15.00
❑ 1995	Supertrucks #17	$1.75

1996

❑ 1996	#1	$2.00
❑ 1996	#87	$2.00
❑ 1996	Black Gold #C1	$10.00
❑ 1996	Black Gold Megaphone XL Die-Cut #JPC2	$10.00
❑ 1996	Black Gold Special Gold #SG1	$40.00
❑ 1996	Gold Signature Series #GS1	$40.00
❑ 1996	Man And Machine #MM1	$8.00

	How Many	Total Value
Page Totals:		

COLLECTOR'S VALUE GUIDE™

1997 Winston Cup Champion Jeff Gordon shows off his trophy on this Press Pass Oil Slick card.

Fleer, cont.	Value
❑ 1996 Ultra Season Crowns #11	$6.00
❑ 1996 Ultra Thunder And Lightning #3	$3.50
❑ 1996 Ultra Thunder And Lightning #4	$3.50
❑ 1996 Ultra Update #12	$2.00
❑ 1996 Ultra Update Autographs #4	$200.00
❑ 1996 Ultra Update Proven Power #4	$48.00
❑ 1996 Ultra Update Winner #1	$4.50
❑ 1996 Ultra Update Winner #4	$4.50
❑ 1996 Ultra Update Winner #10	$4.50

1997

	Value
❑ 1997 Ultra #12	N/E
❑ 1997 Ultra AKA #A2	$50.00
❑ 1997 Ultra Inside Out #DC2	$20.00
❑ 1997 Update Driver View #D1	$15.00
❑ 1997 Update Elite Seats #E1	$22.00

Hi-Tech

1994

	Value
❑ 1994 Brickyard 400 #52	$2.00
❑ 1994 Brickyard 400 #69	$2.00
❑ 1994 Promo #2	$7.00

1995

	Value
❑ 1995 Brickyard 400 #BY1	$2.25

Highland Mint

1994-95

	Value
❑ 1994-95 Jeff Gordon Metallic Bronze	$75.00
❑ 1994-95 Jeff Gordon Metallic Silver	N/E

Maxx

1992

	Value
❑ 1992 Black #29	$4.00
❑ 1992 Red #29	$2.50
❑ 1992 Black Rookie Of The Year #50	$4.00
❑ 1992 Red Rookie Of The Year #50	$2.50

1993

	Value
❑ 1993 #24	$2.00
❑ 1993 #168	$1.25
❑ 1993 Premier Plus #24	$3.50

Flair

1996

	Value
❑ 1996 #12	$3.50
❑ 1996 Autographs #4	$230.00
❑ 1996 Center Spotlight #4	$15.00
❑ 1996 Hot Numbers #3	$50.00
❑ 1996 Power Performance #4	$22.00

Fleer

1996

	Value
❑ 1996 Promo Flair	$12.00
❑ 1996 Promo Ultra w/Blue Foil	$5.00
❑ 1996 Promo Ultra w/Silver Foil	$3.50
❑ 1996 Ultra #1	$2.00
❑ 1996 Ultra #2	$1.75
❑ 1996 Ultra #152	$1.50
❑ 1996 Ultra Autographs	$200.00
❑ 1996 Ultra Champions Club #5	$5.00
❑ 1996 Ultra Flair Preview #1	$16.00
❑ 1996 Ultra Season Crowns #2	$6.00
❑ 1996 Ultra Season Crowns #4	$6.00
❑ 1996 Ultra Season Crowns #7	$6.00
❑ 1996 Ultra Season Crowns #10	$6.00

Page Totals:	How Many	Total Value

Trading Cards

Maxx, cont.

1994

		Value
❑ 1994	#24	$2.00
❑ 1994	Autographs #24	$220.00
❑ 1994	Medallion #1	$1.75
❑ 1994	Medallion #53	$3.00
❑ 1994	Medallion #56	$7.50
❑ 1994	Premier Plus #24	$3.00
❑ 1994	Premier Plus #46	$3.00
❑ 1994	Promo Sample	$10.00
❑ 1994	Rookie Of The Year #16	$6.00
❑ 1994	Winston Cup Rookie Of The Year #201	$2.00
❑ 1994	Winston Select #14	$5.00

1995

		Value
❑ 1995	#24	$2.00
❑ 1995	#236	$2.00
❑ 1995	Autograph #24	$275.00
❑ 1995	Crown Chrome #24	$3.00
❑ 1995	Crown Chrome Pacesetters NNO	$25.00
❑ 1995	Medallion #17	$2.00
❑ 1995	Medallion Puzzle #1-9	$28.00
❑ 1995	Medallion Puzzle #4	$10.00
❑ 1995	Medallion Puzzle Autograph	$240.00
❑ 1995	Medallion On The Road Again #OTR2	$3.00
❑ 1995	Premier Plus #24	$3.25
❑ 1995	Premier Plus Pacesetters #PS7	$22.00
❑ 1995	Promo Gold (foil)	$3.00
❑ 1995	Promo Red (foil)	$5.00

Maxx, cont.

1996

		Value
❑ 1996	#24	$1.75
❑ 1996	Made In America #24	$2.00
❑ 1996	Odyssey #24	$1.75
❑ 1996	Odyssey Millennium #MM6	$4.00
❑ 1996	Premier Series Maxx Autographs #24	$180.00

1997

		Value
❑ 1997	#24	$2.50
❑ 1997	Chase The Champion #C1	$10.00
❑ 1997	First Flags #FF24	$8.00
❑ 1997	Rookie Of The Year #MR6	$15.00

1998

		Value
❑ 1998	#24	$2.50
❑ 1998	10th Anniversary #24	$3.00
❑ 1998	10th Anniversary #124	$3.00
❑ 1998	10th Anniversary #125	$3.00
❑ 1998	10th Anniversary #126	$3.00
❑ 1998	10th Anniversary Buy Back '94 #13 #23	N/E
❑ 1998	10th Anniversary Buy Back Autographs '92 #20	N/E
❑ 1998	10th Anniversary Buy Back Autographs '92 #21	N/E
❑ 1998	10th Anniversary Buy Back Autographs '92 #29	N/E
❑ 1998	10th Anniversary Buy Back Autographs '92 #50	N/E
❑ 1998	10th Anniversary Buy Back Autographs '93 #22	N/E
❑ 1998	10th Anniversary Buy Back Autographs '93 #24	N/E
❑ 1998	10th Anniversary Buy Back Autographs '94 #16	N/E
❑ 1998	10th Anniversary Buy Back Autographs '94 #24	N/E
❑ 1998	10th Anniversary Card Of The Year #CY5	$20.00
❑ 1998	10th Anniversary Card Of The Year #CY10	$20.00
❑ 1998	10th Anniversary Champions Past #CP1	$14.00
❑ 1998	10th Anniversary Maxximum Preview #P24	$5.00
❑ 1998	1997 Year In Review #1	$1.75
❑ 1998	1997 Year In Review #52	$1.75

1999 Wheels High Groove Jeff Gordon pit scene card with special die cut.

Page Totals:	How Many	Total Value

COLLECTOR'S VALUE GUIDE™

1996 Team Pinnacle #1, Jeff Gordon.

Trading Cards

Value

Pinnacle

1995

❑ 1995	Promo #DM8	$16.00
❑ 1995	Promo Select #12	$9.00
❑ 1995	Zenith Championship Quest #78	$3.25
❑ 1995	Zenith Championship Quest #83	$3.25
❑ 1995	Zenith Checklist #77	$1.50
❑ 1995	Zenith End Of The Day #64 .	$3.00
❑ 1995	Zenith Hot Guns #23	$3.00
❑ 1995	Zenith Helmets #3	$80.00
❑ 1995	Zenith Tribute #2	$85.00
❑ 1995	Zenith Winston Winners #2 .	$10.00
❑ 1995	Zenith Winston Winners #4 .	$10.00
❑ 1995	Zenith Winston Winners #6 .	$10.00
❑ 1995	Zenith Winston Winners #15	$10.00
❑ 1995	Zenith Winston Winners #16	$10.00
❑ 1995	Zenith Winston Winners #23	$10.00
❑ 1995	Zenith Z-Team #2	$70.00

1996

❑ 1996	#24	$2.50
❑ 1996	Checkered Flag #1	$25.00
❑ 1996	Cut Above #1	$25.00
❑ 1996	Persistence #66	$1.25
❑ 1996	Persistence #67	$1.25
❑ 1996	Persistence #68	$1.25
❑ 1996	Persistence #69	$1.25
❑ 1996	Persistence #70	$1.25
❑ 1996	Persistence #71	$1.25
❑ 1996	Persistence #72	$1.25
❑ 1996	Persistence #73	$1.25
❑ 1996	Pole Position Certified Strong #1	$30.00
❑ 1996	Pole Position No Limit #1 . .	$32.00
❑ 1996	Pole Position #24	$3.25
❑ 1996	Pole Position #68	$1.50
❑ 1996	Pole Position #69	$1.50
❑ 1996	Pole Position #73	$1.50
❑ 1996	Promo Racer's Choice #9 . . .	$8.00
❑ 1996	Racer's Choice 5x7	$5.00
❑ 1996	Racer's Choice Top Ten #1 .	$24.00

Maxx, cont.   **Value**

❑ 1998	1997 Year In Review #61	$1.75
❑ 1998	1997 Year In Review #71	$1.75
❑ 1998	1997 Year In Review #111 . . .	$1.75
❑ 1998	1997 Year In Review #121 . . .	$1.75
❑ 1998	1997 Year In Review #AW1 . .	$3.00
❑ 1998	1997 Year In Review #PO1 . .	$3.00
❑ 1998	Focus On A Champion #FC1	$24.00
❑ 1998	Promo Maxximum #S24	$5.00
❑ 1998	Teamwork #TW1	$8.00

1999

❑ 1999	#2	$1.25
❑ 1999	Roots of Racing #3	$1.25

Maxximum

1998

❑ 1998	#24	$3.50
❑ 1998	#74	$3.50
❑ 1998	Battle Proven #B5	$8.00
❑ 1998	Field Generals Four Star	N/E
❑ 1998	Field Generals One Star #3 .	$25.00
❑ 1998	Field Generals Three Star Autographs #3	$250.00
❑ 1998	First Class #F1	$7.00

Page Totals:	**How Many**	**Total Value**

Trading Cards

Pinnacle, cont.		Value
1996	Racer's Choice Winston Cup Champion #51	$1.00
1996	Racer's Choice Winston Cup Champion #52	$1.00
1996	Racer's Choice Winston Cup Champion #53	$1.00
1996	Racer's Choice Winston Cup Champion #54	$1.00
1996	Racer's Choice Winston Cup Champion #55	$1.00
1996	Speedflix #9	$1.75
1996	Speedflix #16	$1.75
1996	Speedflix #55	$1.00
1996	Speedflix #56	$1.00
1996	Speedflix #57	$1.00
1996	Speedflix #58	$1.00
1996	Speedflix #59	$1.00
1996	Speedflix #60	$1.00
1996	Speedflix #61	$1.00
1996	Speedflix #62	$1.00
1996	Speedflix #84	$1.25
1996	Speedflix Checklist #86	$1.25
1996	Speedflix Clear Shots #2	$40.00
1996	Speedflix In Motion #2	$27.00
1996	Speedflix ProMotion #2	$15.00
1996	Team Pinnacle #1	$75.00
1996	Team Pinnacle #10	$75.00
1996	Winners #85	$1.25

1997

1997	#24	$3.00
1997	Action Packed Chevy Madness #4	$12.00
1997	Action Packed Promo #8	$3.50
1997	Action Packed Racing #8	$3.00

Jeff Gordon 1997 Rolling Thunder #3 by Action Packed.

Pinnacle, cont.		Value
1997	Action Packed Racing 24KT Gold #3	$100.00
1997	Action Packed Racing Fifth Anniversary #8	$140.00
1997	Action Packed Racing Rolling Thunder #3	$40.00
1997	Certified #24	$5.00
1997	Certified #89	$2.75
1997	Pinnacle Racing #24	$2.75
1997	Pinnacle Racing Chevy Madness #15	$15.00
1997	Pinnacle Racing Spellbound #6-R	$25.00
1997	Pinnacle Racing Spellbound Autographs #6A-R	$190.00
1997	Pinnacle Racing Team Pinnacle #2	$130.00
1997	Precision #3	$12.00
1997	Precision #6	$12.00
1997	Precision #9	$12.00
1997	Racer's Choice #24	$1.75
1997	Racer's Choice Busch Clash #8	$30.00
1997	Racer's Choice High Octane #3	$28.00
1997	Spellbound Autographs Red #6-R	N/E
1997	Totally Certified Platinum Red #24	$10.00

1998

1998	Mint #1	$4.50
1998	Mint #27	$2.00
1998	Mint Championship Mint #1	$22.00
1998	Mint Championship Mint #2	$20.00

Power
1994

1994	#89	$1.25
1994	#90	$1.25

Press Pass
1993

1993	Preview #17	$4.50
1993	Preview Foil #18B	$6.00

Page Totals:	How Many	Total Value

COLLECTOR'S VALUE GUIDE™

1997 Daytona 500 Winner Jeff Gordon holds his trophy in triumph on this SkyBox card.

Press Pass, cont.		Value
❑ 1993	Preview Redemption Expired #18A	$4.00

1994

❑ 1994	#7	$2.00
❑ 1994	Cup Chase #CC7	$22.00
❑ 1994	Optima XL #6	$3.00
❑ 1994	Optima XL #26	$3.00
❑ 1994	Optima XL Promo #3	$10.00
❑ 1994	Optima XL Red Hot #6	$15.00
❑ 1994	Optima XL Red Hot #26	$14.00
❑ 1994	Optima XL Red Hot News Makers #62	$11.00
❑ 1994	Optima XL Red Hot Trophy Case #38	$12.00
❑ 1994	Optima XL Red Hot Winston Cup Scene #56	$11.00
❑ 1994	Promo VIP	$6.00
❑ 1994	Race Day #RD7	$14.00
❑ 1994	VIP #12	$2.00
❑ 1994	VIP 24KT Signature Exchange #EC3	$70.00

1995

❑ 1995	#10	$2.00
❑ 1995	Breaking Through #136	$1.00
❑ 1995	Checkered Flags #CF3	$6.00

Press Pass, cont.		Value
❑ 1995	Cup Chase #10	$30.00
❑ 1995	Optima XL #8	$3.50
❑ 1995	Optima XL JG/XL #1	$6.00
❑ 1995	Optima XL JG/XL #2	$18.00
❑ 1995	Optima XL JG/XL #3	$48.00
❑ 1995	Optima XL JG/XL #4	$180.00
❑ 1995	Optima XL Optima Results #56	$2.25
❑ 1995	Optima XL Stealth #8	$25.00
❑ 1995	Optima XL Trophy Case #31	$2.00
❑ 1995	Premium #8	$3.50
❑ 1995	Premium #33	$3.50
❑ 1995	Premium Hot Pursuit #HP3	$26.00
❑ 1995	Race Day #RD4	$22.00
❑ 1995	Small Town Saturday Night #102	$1.00
❑ 1995	VIP #11	$3.50
❑ 1995	VIP #31	$3.50
❑ 1995	VIP Autographs #11	$225.00
❑ 1995	VIP Emerald Proofs #11	$80.00
❑ 1995	VIP Emerald Proofs #31	$80.00
❑ 1995	VIP Emerald Proofs #61	$40.00
❑ 1995	VIP Fan's Choice #FC3	$15.00
❑ 1995	VIP Helmets #H4	$35.00
❑ 1995	VIP Reflections #R2	$60.00

1996

❑ 1996	#0	$82.00
❑ 1996	#11	$2.00
❑ 1996	#100	$1.50
❑ 1996	Burning Rubber #BR2	$275.00
❑ 1996	Checkered Flags #CF1	$10.00
❑ 1996	Cup Chase #11	$26.00
❑ 1996	Focused #F3	$36.00
❑ 1996	FQS #3A	$15.00
❑ 1996	M-Force #19	$5.00
❑ 1996	M-Force #40	$6.00
❑ 1996	M-Force Blacks #B7	$95.00
❑ 1996	M-Force Promo Blue #1	$7.00
❑ 1996	M-Force Promo Green #2	$7.00
❑ 1996	M-Force Promo Silver #3	$7.00
❑ 1996	M-Force Sheet Metal #5	$350.00
❑ 1996	M-Force Silver #S14	$20.00
❑ 1996	Premium #1	$3.50
❑ 1996	Premium Burning Rubber II #BR1	$285.00
❑ 1996	Premium Crystal Ball #CB5	$25.00
❑ 1996	Premium Hot Pursuit #HP3	$25.00

	How Many	Total Value
Page Totals:		

Trading Cards

	Press Pass, cont.	Value
❏ 1996	Promo Focused #1 .... N/E
❏ 1996	VIP #10 .... $3.00
❏ 1996	VIP #30 .... $2.75
❏ 1996	VIP Autographs #8 ...... $210.00
❏ 1996	VIP Head Gear #HG3 ..... $30.00
❏ 1996	VIP War Paint #WP12 .... $30.00
❏ 1996	Zenith #2 .... $4.00
❏ 1996	Zenith #51 .... $2.00
❏ 1996	Zenith #73 .... $2.00
❏ 1996	Zenith #80 .... $2.00
❏ 1996	Zenith #91 .... $2.00
❏ 1996	Zenith #92 .... $2.00
❏ 1996	Zenith #98 .... $2.00
❏ 1996	Zenith #99 Checklist $2.00
❏ 1996	Zenith Champion Salute #1 .... $80.00
❏ 1996	Zenith Highlights #2 ...... $15.00

1997

		Value
❏ 1997	#2 .... $2.25
❏ 1997	Activision Autographs ... $275.00
❏ 1997	Activision Pit Stop #10 .... $10.00
❏ 1997	Activision w/Craven and Labonte $10.00
❏ 1997	Activision #5 w/Labonte and Wallace $10.00
❏ 1997	Banquet Bound #2 .... $10.00
❏ 1997	Burning Rubber #5 ...... $275.00
❏ 1997	Clear Cut #2 .... $18.00
❏ 1997	Cup Chase #7 .... $45.00
❏ 1997	Premium #2 .... $3.50
❏ 1997	Premium #38 .... $3.50
❏ 1997	Premium Autographs $275.00
❏ 1997	Premium Crystal Ball #CB4 .... $20.00

1993 Rookie of the Year Jeff Gordon playfully kisses his trophy on this Action Packed card.

	Press Pass, cont.	Value
❏ 1997	Premium Double Burners #DB2 .... $290.00
❏ 1997	Premium Lap Leaders #LL3 . $15.00
❏ 1997	Premium Promo #1 .... $7.00
❏ 1997	Sam Bass #SB1 .... $80.00
❏ 1997	VIP #8 .... $3.25
❏ 1997	VIP Head Gear #HG3 ..... $20.00
❏ 1997	VIP Precious Metal SM1 . $325.00
❏ 1997	VIP Ring Of Honor #RH8 .. $18.00
❏ 1997	VIP Sam Bass #2 .... N/E
❏ 1997	Victory Lane #2A $20.00

1998

		Value
❏ 1998	#1 .... $2.00
❏ 1998	#101 .... $3.25
❏ 1998	1997 Champion #0 ...... $85.00
❏ 1998	Autographs #2 .... $250.00
❏ 1998	Cup Chase #CC7 .... $50.00
❏ 1998	Oil Cans #OC3 .... $25.00
❏ 1998	Pit Stop #PS12 .... $15.00
❏ 1998	Premium #28 .... $5.00
❏ 1998	Premium Flag Chasers #FC1 . $7.00
❏ 1998	Premium Promo #1 .... $6.00
❏ 1998	Premium Rivalries #R1B .. $10.00
❏ 1998	Premium Steel Horses #SH7 .... $14.00
❏ 1998	Premium Triple Gear Fire Suit #TGF6 .... $350.00
❏ 1998	Promo #1 .... $4.00
❏ 1998	Promo Stealth #1 .... $4.00
❏ 1998	Race Used Gloves #G6 ... $325.00
❏ 1998	Shockers Hobby #ST2A $25.00
❏ 1998	Signings Gold #1 .... $300.00
❏ 1998	Signings PPP/VIP/S #1 ... $200.00
❏ 1998	Stealth #10 .... $4.00
❏ 1998	Stealth Awards #5 ...... $52.00
❏ 1998	Stealth Awards #7 .... $110.00
❏ 1998	Stealth Champ Bronze #0 . .$25.00
❏ 1998	Stealth Champ Gold #0 .. $80.00
❏ 1998	Stealth Champ Silver #0 .. $45.00
❏ 1998	Stealth Fan Talk #3 .... $10.00
❏ 1998	Stealth Octane #13 .... $6.00
❏ 1998	Stealth Octane #14 ..... $5.00
❏ 1998	Stealth Race Used Glove #G6 .... $325.00
❏ 1998	Stealth Stars #5 .... $14.00
❏ 1998	Stealth Teammates #47 .... $4.00

Page Totals:	How Many	Total Value

COLLECTOR'S
VALUE GUIDE™

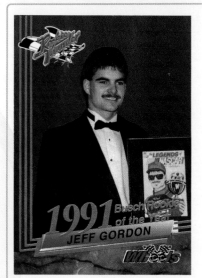

Jeff Gordon's 1991 Busch Rookie of the Year honor is portrayed on this Wheels Rookie Thunder card.

Trading Cards

Press Pass, cont.		Value
❏ 1998	Torpedoes Ring Of Honor #ST2B	$13.00
❏ 1998	Triple Gear 3 In 1 Redemption #STG6	$840.00
❏ 1998	Triple Gear Burning Rubber #TG6	$225.00
❏ 1998	VIP #8	$3.25
❏ 1998	VIP Driving Force #DF7	$10.00
❏ 1998	VIP Head Gear #HG4	$13.00
❏ 1998	VIP Lap Leader #LL3	$13.00
❏ 1998	VIP NASCAR Country #NC3	$12.00
❏ 1998	VIP Triple Gear Sheet Metal #TGS6	$260.00

1999

❏ 1999	#1	$2.00
❏ 1999	Burning Rubber #BR7	$210.00
❏ 1999	Chase Cars #11B	$14.00
❏ 1999	Cup Chase #6	$30.00
❏ 1999	On The Pole #79	$2.00
❏ 1999	Oil Cans #6	$18.00
❏ 1999	Pit Stop #12	$10.00
❏ 1999	Premium #8	$4.00
❏ 1999	Premium Badge Of Honor #BH10	$9.00

Press Pass, cont.		Value
❏ 1999	Premium Badge Of Honor #BH24	$5.00
❏ 1999	Premium Burning Desire #FD1B	$55.00
❏ 1999	Premium Extreme Fire #FD1A	$55.00
❏ 1999	Premium Race-Used Fire Suit #F1	$240.00
❏ 1999	Premium Steel Horses #SH9	$14.00
❏ 1999	Promo	$4.00
❏ 1999	Retro #101	$2.75
❏ 1999	Showman #11A	$23.00
❏ 1999	Signings/400 #17	$275.00
❏ 1999	Signings Gold/100 #4	$300.00
❏ 1999	Stealth #10	$3.50
❏ 1999	Stealth Big Numbers BN7	$5.00
❏ 1999	Stealth Big Numbers BN8	$5.00
❏ 1999	Stealth Headlines #SH1	$45.00
❏ 1999	Stealth Octane SLX #06	$4.00
❏ 1999	Stealth Octane SLX #07	$4.00
❏ 1999	Stealth Race SST #SS3	$18.00
❏ 1999	Stealth Race Used Glove #G2	$360.00
❏ 1999	Triple Gear 3 In 1 Redemption #TG3	$800.00
❏ 1999	VIP #8	$2.75
❏ 1999	VIP #31	$2.75
❏ 1999	VIP BGN #31	$2.75
❏ 1999	VIP Double Take #DT1	$14.00
❏ 1999	VIP Head Gear #HG1	$9.00
❏ 1999	VIP Lap Leader #LL1	$14.00
❏ 1999	VIP Out Of The Box #OB1	$9.00
❏ 1999	VIP Rear View Mirror #RM1	$5.00
❏ 1999	VIP Sheet Metal #SM3	$240.00
❏ 1999	Winston Cup Preview #99	$2.00

2000

❏ 2000	#6	$2.00
❏ 2000	#53	$2.00
❏ 2000	#63	$2.00
❏ 2000	Burning Rubber #BR5	$225.00
❏ 2000	Cup Chase #CC6	$45.00
❏ 2000	Gatorade Front Runner	N/E
❏ 2000	Oil Cans #OC6	$12.00
❏ 2000	Signings TRADE #6	$250.00
❏ 2000	Skidmarks #SK5	$32.00
❏ 2000	Techno-Retro #TR8	$2.00

Page Totals:	How Many	Total Value

Trading Cards

Pro Set

1992

		Value
❏ 1992	#128	$2.75

1994

| ❏ 1994 | Promo Power | $6.00 |

Quik Chek

1993

| ❏ 1993 | Jeff Gordon Metallic | $16.00 |

Score Board

1997

❏ 1997	Autographed Racing #4	$2.00
❏ 1997	Autographed Racing #41	$2.00
❏ 1997	Autographed Racing Autographs #16	$225.00
❏ 1997	Autographed Racing Mayne St. #KM4	$14.00
❏ 1997	Autographed Racing Take The Checkered Flag #TF1	$100.00
❏ 1997	Motorsports #2	$1.75
❏ 1997	Motorsports Autographs #AU2	$290.00
❏ 1997	Racing IQ #2	$4.00
❏ 1997	Racing IQ #26	$4.00
❏ 1997	Racing IQ #37	$4.00
❏ 1997	Racing IQ Sam Bass #SB2	$172.00

Select

1995

❏ 1995	#12	$2.50
❏ 1995	Dream Machines #DM8	$42.00
❏ 1995	Jumbo	$15.00

1995 Jeff Gordon Crown Jewels Signature Gem Card.

Select, cont.

		Value
❏ 1995	Pole Sitters #141	$1.75
❏ 1995	Select Skills #SS3	$25.00
❏ 1995	Young Stars #118	$1.75

SkyBox

1994

| ❏ 1994 | #4 | $2.50 |

1997

❏ 1997	Profile #7	$4.00
❏ 1997	Profile Promo	$3.50
❏ 1997	Profile Racing Autographs #7	$290.00
❏ 1997	Profile Racing Break Out #B1	$10.00
❏ 1997	Profile Racing Daytona #D1	N/E
❏ 1997	Profile Racing Pace Setters #E5	$13.00
❏ 1997	Profile Racing Team #T2	$100.00

Traks

1991

| ❏ 1991 | #1 | $12.00 |

1992

| ❏ 1992 | #101 | $2.50 |
| ❏ 1992 | Autographs #A7 | $120.00 |

1993

❏ 1993	#39	$2.00
❏ 1993	#151	$7.50
❏ 1993	First Run #39	$3.00
❏ 1993	Promo	$7.50

1994

❏ 1994	#36	$2.25
❏ 1994	8x10 Art Cards Set Of 5	$4.00
❏ 1994	Autographs #A2	$27.00
❏ 1994	Autographs #A4	$100.00
❏ 1994	First Run #24	$3.75
❏ 1994	First Run #36	$3.50
❏ 1994	First Run #86	$3.50
❏ 1994	First Run #106	$3.50
❏ 1994	First Run #171	$3.50

1995

❏ 1995	#4	$1.75
❏ 1995	#26	$1.75
❏ 1995	#52	$1.75
❏ 1995	#58	$1.75

Page Totals:	How Many	Total Value

COLLECTOR'S VALUE GUIDE™

Jeff Gordon on the 1995 Crown Jewels Sapphire card, 1 of 2500.

Traks, cont.

		Value
❑ 1995	#68	$1.75
❑ 1995	Challenger Series #C1	$45.00
❑ 1995	Promo First Run #26	$4.00
❑ 1995	Racing Machines #RM7	$21.00
❑ 1995	Series Stars #SS8	$16.00
❑ 1995	Visions #E1	$15.00
❑ 1995	Visions 5th Anniversary #4	$2.00
❑ 1995	Visions 5th Anniversary #38	$2.00
❑ 1995	Visions 5th Anniversary Clear Contenders #C3	$9.00
❑ 1995	Visions 5th Anniversary Retrospective #R3	$7.00

1996

		Value
❑ 1996	Review/Preview #15	$1.75
❑ 1996	Review/Preview Liquid Gold #LG18	$25.00

Upper Deck

1995

		Value
❑ 1995	#2	$2.75
❑ 1995	#202	$2.75
❑ 1995	#246	$1.50
❑ 1995	5x7 Cards #OS3	$10.00
❑ 1995	Autographs #202	$285.00
❑ 1995	Illustrations #19	$12.00

Upper Deck, cont.

		Value
❑ 1995	Predictor Points #PP6	$10.00
❑ 1995	Predictor Race Winners #P4	$12.00
❑ 1995	SP #55	$3.00
❑ 1995	SP #56	$3.00
❑ 1995	SP Cup Contenders #18	$3.50
❑ 1995	SP Promo #JG1	N/E
❑ 1995	SP Speed Merchants #SM24	$14.00

1996

		Value
❑ 1996	#22	$2.00
❑ 1996	All-Pro #AP1	$30.00
❑ 1996	Predictor Poles #RP1	$10.00
❑ 1996	Predictor Wins #HP1	$12.00
❑ 1996	Road To The Cup #RC1	$2.50
❑ 1996	Road To The Cup #RC121	$2.50
❑ 1996	Road To The Cup #RC124	$2.50
❑ 1996	Road To The Cup #RC148	$2.50
❑ 1996	Road To The Cup Autographs #H1	$250.00
❑ 1996	Road To The Cup Leaders Of The Pack #LP1	$20.00
❑ 1996	Road To The Cup Predictor Points #PP1	$17.00
❑ 1996	SP #24	$4.00
❑ 1996	SP #43 Cup Contenders	$3.50
❑ 1996	SP #80 RPM	$3.50
❑ 1996	SP Holoview Maximum Effects #ME1	$28.00
❑ 1996	SP Racing Legends #24	$25.00
❑ 1996	SPx #1	$12.00
❑ 1996	SPx Auto #T1A	$250.00
❑ 1996	SPx Elite #E1	$54.00
❑ 1996	SPx Promo #1	$10.00
❑ 1996	SPx Tribute #T1	$50.00
❑ 1996	Virtual Velocity #W1	$10.00

1997

		Value
❑ 1997	Collector's Choice #24	$1.75
❑ 1997	Collector's Choice 5x7 Dynamic Debut	$7.00
❑ 1997	Collector's Choice 5x7 Magic Memories	$7.00
❑ 1997	Collector's Choice Checklist #154	$1.00
❑ 1997	Collector's Choice Triple Force #F1	$10.00

Page Totals:	How Many	Total Value

Trading Cards

	Upper Deck, cont.		Value
❑	1997	Collector's Choice Triple Force #G2	$10.00
❑	1997	Collector's Choice Triple Force #G3	$10.00
❑	1997	Collector's Choice Victory Circle #2	$38.00
❑	1997	Promo SPx #1	$10.00
❑	1997	Road To The Cup #2	$2.00
❑	1997	Road To The Cup #87	$2.00
❑	1997	Road To The Cup Quest #2	$25.00
❑	1997	Road To The Cup Million Dollar Memoirs #MM5	N/E
❑	1997	Road To The Cup Million Dollar Memoirs Autographs #MM6	N/E
❑	1997	Road To The Cup Million Dollar Memoirs Autographs #MM7	N/E
❑	1997	Road To The Cup Piece Of The Action Harness	$275.00
❑	1997	Road To The Cup Piece Of The Action Net	$275.00
❑	1997	Road To The Cup Piece Of The Action Seat	$275.00
❑	1997	Road To The Cup Predictor Plus #2	$8.00
❑	1997	Road To The Cup Predictor Plus #11	$8.00
❑	1997	Road To The Cup Predictor Plus #28	$8.00
❑	1997	Road To The Cup Premier Position	$9.00
❑	1997	SP #66	$2.00

Jeff Gordon 1997 Fleer Ultra Update Driver View die-cut racing card #D1

	Upper Deck, cont.		Value
❑	1997	SP 2Flag #102	$17.00
❑	1997	SP 3Flag #24	$35.00
❑	1997	SP 3Flag #122	$35.00
❑	1997	SP Promo #S24	N/E
❑	1997	SP Race Film #RD1	$170.00
❑	1997	SPx #24	$7.00
❑	1997	SPx Force Autographs #SF1	N/E
❑	1997	SPx SpeedView Artifacts #SV1	N/E
❑	1997	SPx Tag Team #TT1	N/E
❑	1997	SPx Tag Team Autographs TA1	N/E
❑	1997	Victory Circle #24	$2.00
❑	1997	Victory Circle #111	$2.00
❑	1997	Victory Circle Championship Reflections #CR2	$7.00
❑	1997	Victory Circle Driver's Seat #DS2	$40.00
❑	1997	Victory Circle Generation Excitement #GE1	$12.00
❑	1997	Victory Circle Piece Of The Action #FS1	$325.00
❑	1997	Victory Circle Piece Of The Action #FS2	$250.00
❑	1997	Victory Circle Piece Of The Action #FS3	$220.00
❑	1997	Victory Circle Predictor #PE1	$22.00
❑	1997	Victory Circle Victory Lap #VL2	$105.00

1998

			Value
❑	1998	Collector's Choice #24	$1.50
❑	1998	Collector's Choice Star Quest Autographs #SQ41	$180.00
❑	1998	Collector's Choice Star Quest Win #SQ36	$40.00
❑	1998	Diamond Vision #RT1	N/E
❑	1998	Diamond Vision Vision Of A Champion #VC3	$38.00
❑	1998	Road To The Cup #24	$4.00
❑	1998	Road To The Cup #66	$4.00
❑	1998	Road To The Cup 50th Anniversary #AN43	$7.00
❑	1998	Road To The Cup 50th Anniversary Autographs Red #AN47	$400.00
❑	1998	Road To The Cup Cover Story #CS8	$7.00

Page Totals:	How Many	Total Value

Trading Cards

1975 Jeff Gordon at 3 years of age, Maxx 1993

AGE 3 • 1975

Upper Deck, cont.		Value
❑ 1998	Road To The Cup Cover Story #CS13	$7.00
❑ 1998	Road To The Cup Cup Quest Turn 1 #CQ1	$18.00
❑ 1998	SP Authentics #24	$4.50
❑ 1998	SP Authentics #72	$4.50
❑ 1998	SP Authentics Behind The Wheel #BW1	$9.00
❑ 1998	SP Authentics Sign Of The Times Level 2 #ST1	$250.00
❑ 1998	SP Authentics Traditions #T2 Red	$375.00
❑ 1998	Victory Circle #24	$4.50
❑ 1998	Victory Circle #92	$3.00
❑ 1998	Victory Circle #100	$4.50
❑ 1998	Victory Circle #105	$4.50
❑ 1998	Victory Circle #119	$4.50
❑ 1998	Victory Circle #120	$4.50
❑ 1998	Victory Circle 32 Days Of Speed #D2	$6.00
❑ 1998	Victory Circle 32 Days Of Speed #D11	$6.00
❑ 1998	Victory Circle 32 Days Of Speed #D32	$6.00

Upper Deck, cont.		Value
❑ 1998	Victory Circle Autographs #AG1	$275.00
❑ 1998	Victory Circle Point Leaders #PL1	$18.00
❑ 1998	Victory Circle Sparks Of Brilliance #SB1	$90.00

1999

❑ 1999	Maxx #1	$2.25
❑ 1999	Maxx FANtastic Finishes #F1	$15.00
❑ 1999	Maxx Focus On A Champ #FC1	$24.00
❑ 1999	Maxx Race Ticket #RT22	$10.00
❑ 1999	Maxx Racer's Ink #JG	$400.00
❑ 1999	Maxx Racing Images #RI24	$4.50
❑ 1999	Road To The Cup #24	$2.25
❑ 1999	Road To The Cup #61	$2.00
❑ 1999	Road To The Cup #RTTC1	$12.00
❑ 1999	Road To The Cup NASCAR Chronicles #NC2	$5.00
❑ 1999	Road To The Cup Profiles #P15	$14.00
❑ 1999	Road To The Cup Signature Collection	N/E
❑ 1999	Road To The Cup Signed Tires Of Daytona #TS1	N/E
❑ 1999	SP Authentics #1	$4.00
❑ 1999	SP Authentics CLASS #65	$4.00
❑ 1999	SP Authentics Cup Challengers #CC1	$17.00
❑ 1999	SP Authentics Driving Force #DF8	$9.00
❑ 1999	SP Authentics In The Driver's Seat #DS10	$5.00
❑ 1999	SP Authentics Overdrive #82	$16.00
❑ 1999	SP Authentics Sign Of The Times #9	$210.00
❑ 1999	Victory Circle #3	$2.50
❑ 1999	Victory Circle #76	$2.50
❑ 1999	Victory Circle #84	$2.50
❑ 1999	Victory Circle #V8	$25.00
❑ 1999	Victory Circle Income Statement #IS1	$5.00
❑ 1999	Victory Circle NASCAR Signature Collection #JG	N/E

Page Totals:	How Many	Total Value

Trading Cards

Upper Deck, cont.		Value
☐ 1999	Victory Circle Speedzone #SZ3	$5.00
☐ 1999	Victory Circle Track Masters #TM1	$14.00

2000

☐ 2000	MVP #24	$2.25
☐ 2000	MVP #65	$1.50
☐ 2000	MVP Cup Quest 2000 #CQ9	$3.50
☐ 2000	MVP Legends In The Making #LM1	$4.00
☐ 2000	MVP NASCAR Gallery #NG9	$10.00
☐ 2000	MVP NASCAR Stars 2000 #NS2	$4.00
☐ 2000	MVP Pro Sign 2000 Red #PSJG	$140.00
☐ 2000	Victory Circle #16	$2.00
☐ 2000	Victory Circle #73	$1.25
☐ 2000	Victory Circle Income Statement #IS1	$4.00
☐ 2000	Victory Circle NASCAR Signature Collection Red #JG	N/E
☐ 2000	Victory Circle Powerdeck #PD5	$80.00
☐ 2000	Victory Circle Winning Material #TJG	N/E

Wheels

1993

☐ 1993	Promo Rookie Thunder #P2	$9.00
☐ 1993	Rookie Thunder #32	$1.25
☐ 1993	Rookie Thunder #37	$1.25
☐ 1993	Rookie Thunder #50	$1.25

1998 Jeff Gordon Press Pass Premium driver's dashboard view die-cut card.

Wheels, cont.		Value
☐ 1993	Rookie Thunder #51	$1.25
☐ 1993	Rookie Thunder #62	$1.25
☐ 1993	Rookie Thunder #70	$1.25
☐ 1993	Rookie Thunder #71	$1.25
☐ 1993	Rookie Thunder #82	$1.25
☐ 1993	Rookie Thunder #97	$1.25
☐ 1993	Rookie Thunder #98	$1.25

1994

☐ 1994	Farewell Tour Promo	N/E
☐ 1994	Harry Gant #66	$2.00
☐ 1994	High Gear #101	$2.25
☐ 1994	High Gear Day One #101	$3.50
☐ 1994	High Gear Dominators #D5	$35.00
☐ 1994	High Gear Gold #73	$7.00
☐ 1994	High Gear Mega Gold #MG5	$16.00
☐ 1994	High Gear Promo #P1	$10.00
☐ 1994	High Gear Promo Gold Foil #P1	$19.00
☐ 1994	High Gear Rookie Thunder Update #102	$5.00
☐ 1994	High Gear Winston Cup Rookie Of The Year	$2.25
☐ 1994	Promo Harry Gant Set	$8.00

1995

☐ 1995	Crown Jewels #2	$2.50
☐ 1995	Crown Jewels #75	$2.25
☐ 1995	Crown Jewels #77	$2.25
☐ 1995	Crown Jewels Dual Jewels #1	$42.00
☐ 1995	Crown Jewels Signature Gems #1	$30.00
☐ 1995	High Gear #6	$2.00
☐ 1995	High Gear Busch Clash #BC7	$10.00
☐ 1995	High Gear Promo #P2	$7.00
☐ 1995	High Gear Race Winner #91	$1.50
☐ 1995	Promo Crown Jewels Diamond #P1	$33.00
☐ 1995	Promo Crown Jewels Emerald #P1	$25.00
☐ 1995	Promo Crown Jewels Ruby #P1	$10.00

1996

☐ 1996	Crown Jewels Elite #2	$2.00

Page Totals:	How Many	Total Value

COLLECTOR'S
VALUE GUIDE™

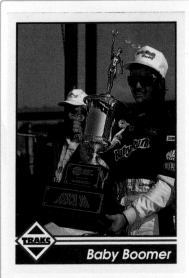

Baby Boomer

Jeff Gordon met with success in his Baby Ruth Ford as shown on this 1992 Traks card.

	Wheels, cont.		Value
❏	1996	Crown Jewels Elite #28	$2.00
❏	1996	Crown Jewels Elite #29	$2.00
❏	1996	Crown Jewels Elite #30	$2.00
❏	1996	Crown Jewels Elite Diamond Elite Crown Signature Amethyst #CS2	$32.00
❏	1996	Crown Jewels Elite Dual Jewels Amethyst #DJ1	$34.00
❏	1996	Crown Jewels Elite Dual Jewels Garnet #DJ1	$28.00
❏	1996	Crown Jewels Elite Sapphire #DJ1	$70.00
❏	1996	Knightquest #2	$2.00
❏	1996	Knightquest #21	$2.00
❏	1996	Knightquest #30	$2.00
❏	1996	Knightquest #31	$2.00
❏	1996	Knightquest First Knights #FK3	$22.00
❏	1996	Knightquest Knights Of The Round Table #KT1	$48.00
❏	1996	Knightquest Protectors Of The Crown #PC6	$70.00
❏	1996	Race Sharks Promo #P1	N/E
❏	1996	Viper #2	$2.00
❏	1996	Viper #40	$2.00

	Wheels, cont.		Value
❏	1996	Viper #42	$2.00
❏	1996	Viper Busch Clash #B5	$20.00
❏	1996	Viper Cobra #C2	$28.00
❏	1996	Viper Diamondback #D1	$40.00
❏	1996	Viper Diamondback Authentic #DA1	$115.00
❏	1996	Viper King Cobra #KC2	$40.00
❏	1996	Viper Promo #P3	$18.00

1997

			Value
❏	1997	Black Wolf Promo #P3	$10.00
❏	1997	Jurassic Park #1	$2.75
❏	1997	Jurassic Park #48	$2.75
❏	1997	Jurassic Park #51	$2.75
❏	1997	Jurassic Park Carnivores #C2	$25.00
❏	1997	Jurassic Park Pteranodon #P2	$30.00
❏	1997	Jurassic Park T-Rex TR2	$80.00
❏	1997	Jurassic Park Thunder Lizards TL1	$110.00
❏	1997	Jurassic Park Raptors #R2	$15.00
❏	1997	Predator #1	$2.50
❏	1997	Predator #74	$2.50
❏	1997	Predator American Eagle #AE2	$36.00
❏	1997	Predator Eye Of The Tiger #ET2	$14.00
❏	1997	Predator Gatorbacks #GB2	$38.00
❏	1997	Predator Golden Eagle #GE2	$38.00
❏	1997	Predator Promo #P1	$9.00
❏	1997	Race Sharks #2	$2.50
❏	1997	Race Sharks #35	$2.50
❏	1997	Race Sharks #36	$2.50
❏	1997	Race Sharks #40	$2.50
❏	1997	Race Sharks #43	$2.50
❏	1997	Race Sharks First Bite Shark Attack Preview 5x7 #SA2	$15.00
❏	1997	Race Sharks Great White #GW2	$75.00
❏	1997	Race Sharks Shark Attack #SA2	$40.00
❏	1997	Race Sharks Shark Tooth Signature #ST2	$250.00
❏	1997	Red Wolf Promo #P2	$10.00
❏	1997	Viper #51	$2.50
❏	1997	Viper Anaconda #A2	$30.00

Page Totals:	How Many	Total Value

Trading Cards

Wheels, cont.

			Value
❑	1997	Viper Cobra #C2	$25.00
❑	1997	Viper Diamondback #DB1	$40.00
❑	1997	Viper King Cobra #KC2	$40.00
❑	1997	Viper Promo #P2	N/E
❑	1997	Viper Sidewinder #S2	$15.00
❑	1997	Viper Snake Eyes #SE2	$20.00

1998

❑	1998	#11	$2.00
❑	1998	#85	$2.00
❑	1998	50th Anniversary #A5	$7.00
❑	1998	Autographs #2	$195.00
❑	1998	Custom Shop Redemption #CSJG	$150.00
❑	1998	Double Take #E4	$65.00
❑	1998	Green Flags #GF6	$15.00
❑	1998	High Gear #1	$2.50
❑	1998	High Gear #50	$2.50
❑	1998	High Gear Autographs #8	$300.00
❑	1998	High Gear Custom Shop Redemption #CS2	$150.00
❑	1998	High Gear Gear Jammers #GJ12	$7.00
❑	1998	High Gear High Groove #HG5	$9.00
❑	1998	High Gear Man And Machine #MM1A	$15.00
❑	1998	High Gear Man And Machine #MM1B	$21.00
❑	1998	High Gear Pure Gold #PG3	$9.00
❑	1998	High Gear Top Tier #TT1	$125.00
❑	1998	Jackpot #J3	$15.00

Jeff Gordon's Chroma Premier car, 1997 Upper Deck Road To The Cup Million Dollar Memoirs.

Wheels, cont.

1999

			Value
❑	1999	#12	$2.50
❑	1999	#42	$2.50
❑	1999	Autographs #8	$265.00
❑	1999	Circuit Breakers #CB5	$24.00
❑	1999	Custom Shop Redemption #CS2	$88.00
❑	1999	Daytona Seven Flag Chasers Checkered #DS1	$225.00
❑	1999	Dialed In #D1	$12.00
❑	1999	High Gear #46	$2.50
❑	1999	High Gear #54	$2.50
❑	1999	High Gear #58	$2.50
❑	1999	High Gear Custom Shop #CSJG	$90.00
❑	1999	High Gear Daytona #0	N/E
❑	1999	High Gear Daytona #1	N/E
❑	1999	High Gear Flag Chasers #FC1	$220.00
❑	1999	High Gear Gear Shifters #GS1	$7.00
❑	1999	High Gear Man And Machine #MM1A	$18.00
❑	1999	High Gear Man And Machine #MM1B	$14.00
❑	1999	High Gear Promo	N/E
❑	1999	High Gear Top Tier #TT1	$120.00
❑	1999	High Groove #HG3	$9.00
❑	1999	High Groove #HG7	$9.00
❑	1999	Hot Streaks #HS1	$8.00
❑	1999	Runnin And Gunnin #RG9	$5.00
❑	1999	Runnin And Gunnin #RG18	$30.00

2000

❑	2000	#41	$2.00
❑	2000	#48	$2.00
❑	2000	#59	$2.00
❑	2000	Custom Shop #CSJG	$90.00
❑	2000	Flag Chasers #FC2	$200.00
❑	2000	Gear Shifters #GS6	$4.00
❑	2000	High Gear #33	$2.00
❑	2000	Man And Machine #MM6A	$5.00
❑	2000	Man And Machine #MM6B	$3.50
❑	2000	Sunday Sensation #OC6	N/E
❑	2000	Top Tier #TT4	$90.00
❑	2000	Winning Edge #BR5	N/E

Page Totals:	How Many	Total Value

COLLECTOR'S
VALUE GUIDE™

Future Releases

Use this page to record future Jeff Gordon releases.

Jeff Gordon	Value	How Many	Total Value

Page Totals:	How Many	Total Value

Future Releases

Use this page to record future Jeff Gordon releases.

Jeff Gordon	Value	How Many	Total Value

Page Totals:	How Many	Total Value

Total Value Of My Collection

Record your collection here by adding the totals from the bottom of each Value Guide page.

Die-Cast Cars		
Page Number	How Many	Total Value
Page 33		
Page 34		
Page 35		
Page 36		
Page 37		
Page 38		
Page 39		
Page 40		
Page 41		
Page 42		
Page 43		
Page 44		
Page 45		
Page 46		
Page 47		
Page 48		
Page 49		
Page 50		
Page 51		
Page 52		
Page 53		
Page 54		
Page 55		
Page 56		
Page 57		
Subtotal		

Die-Cast Cars, Cont.		
Page Number	How Many	Total Value
Page 58		
Page 59		
Page 60		
Page 61		
Page 62		
Page 63		
Page 64		

Banks		
Page 65		
Page 66		
Page 67		
Page 68		
Page 69		
Page 70		
Page 71		
Page 72		
Page 73		
Page 74		
Page 75		
Page 76		
Page 77		
Page 78		
Page 79		
Page 80		
Page 81		
Subtotal		

Page Totals:	How Many	Total Value

Total Value Of My Collection

Record your collection here by adding the totals from the bottom of each Value Guide page.

Banks, Cont.		
Page Number	How Many	Total Value
Page 82		
Commemorative Cars		
Page 83		
Page 84		
Page 85		
Crystal Cars		
Page 85		
Page 86		
Duallies		
Page 87		
Page 88		
Page 89		
Page 90		
Helmets		
Page 91		
Page 92		
Pit Scenes		
Page 93		
Page 94		
Page 95		
Sets		
Page 96		
Page 97		
Page 98		
Page 99		
Page 100		
Subtotal		

Sets, Cont.		
Page Number	How Many	Total Value
Page 101		
Page 102		
Suburbans		
Page 103		
Transporters		
Page 104		
Page 105		
Trading Cards		
Page 106		
Page 107		
Page 108		
Page 109		
Page 110		
Page 111		
Page 112		
Page 113		
Page 114		
Page 115		
Page 116		
Page 117		
Page 118		
Page 119		
Page 120		
Page 121		
Page 122		
Subtotal		

Grand Total	How Many	Total Value

Secondary Market Overview

Finding the Jeff Gordon collectible you desire may seem like a difficult journey. Many pieces speed off store shelves the minute they arrive. But with these helpful hints, you should be well on your way to the winner's circle of collecting!

There are an almost limitless number of collectibles that honor Gordon. Some are fairly common and can be found in most department stores. But for items such as die-cast, which often have limited production runs, you may have to consider other options.

Not everybody can live near a NASCAR racetrack and buy Gordon merchandise there. Luckily, racing stores are becoming a common sight all over the country. These stores tend to carry die-cast, trading cards and apparel for the most popular drivers. If you don't have a store like that in your area, baseball card stores can also be good place to look for Gordon merchandise.

Model and hobby stores often carry a selection of die-cast cars. If they don't have the car you are looking for, they may be able to put you in touch with a fellow die-cast collector who would be willing to trade with you.

The Internet a very useful tool for connecting you with NASCAR fans and stores all over the country. Simply typing "Jeff Gordon" into an Internet search engine will point you in the direction of many retail and fan sites devoted to Gordon. These web sites may even introduce you to Gordon merchandise you never knew existed. Good luck and happy collecting!

Other Jeff Gordon®
Products And Accessories

There is so much more Jeff Gordon memorabilia to collect than just die-cast products. From posters and puzzles to pins and plush figures, there are Rainbow Warrior–inspired products to wear, play with, display in your house and even eat! You can show that Gordon is your favorite race car driver by using #24 mouse pads, clocks and lighters, wearing his caps, T-shirts and watches or purchasing food that has his smiling face on the containers.

We haven't assigned any secondary market values to these products, but that doesn't mean that they aren't valuable. Some of the memorabilia found on these pages can fetch fairly high prices on the secondary market. Check with your local dealers to find out what your collection is worth.

Action Figures

Action figures aren't just for kids anymore! With the help of manufacturers like Kenner, figures such as those in the Starting Lineup series have become a fun collectible for serious race fans as well. Gordon action figures feature the Wonder Boy in a variety of outfits, such as sporting a Pepsi driving suit or the colorful DuPont

uniform. One of the most valuable action figures on the secondary market is a 12-inch Kenner special edition that can command in the $100 price range! Most action figures, however, can be found for around $20 in department stores and hobby shops.

Baseballs

It's impossible to strike out with a Jeff Gordon baseball. A unique combination of two favorite American sports, this baseball is officially licensed by NASCAR and is made by ProBall, Inc., which began the RaceBalls line in 1997. The baseball comes in a clear plastic cover mounted on a stand designed to look like a car tire. The Jeff Gordon ball is imprinted with #24 as well as a replication of Gordon's famous signature. Appropriately, it is decorated with Gordon's trademark rainbow colors. Get yours now before they are going, going, gone!

Belt Buckles

Americraft Pewter Accessories and Montana Silversmiths produce a variety of Jeff Gordon belt buckles, all of which are officially licensed by NASCAR. Americraft buckles feature a Gordon theme on their front and a short write-up about him on their back. They currently offer more than 40 different buckles. The Montana collection offers buckles in many different shapes and sizes to accentuate formal or casual attire. Most buckles sell in the $15 to $20 range and are available through hobby shops that sell NASCAR merchandise or trackside vendors.

Beverage Containers

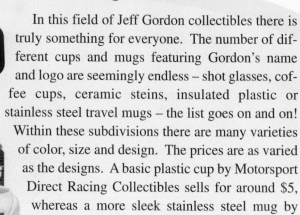

In this field of Jeff Gordon collectibles there is truly something for everyone. The number of different cups and mugs featuring Gordon's name and logo are seemingly endless – shot glasses, coffee cups, ceramic steins, insulated plastic or stainless steel travel mugs – the list goes on and on! Within these subdivisions there are many varieties of color, size and design. The prices are as varied as the designs. A basic plastic cup by Motorsport Direct Racing Collectibles sells for around $5, whereas a more sleek stainless steel mug by Racing USA costs about $25.

Cereal Boxes

The most important meal of the day and the (arguably) most important man in racing have joined forces! Jeff Gordon's face has graced the front of close to 20 cereal boxes over the last several years. Kellogg's, one of the leading promoters of NASCAR in the cereal world, has put Gordon's image on boxes of their cereal. The size, color and design of the boxes are subject to change from series to series. Collectors can either leave the cereal boxes unopened or remove the cereal and fill them up with crumpled paper for a fuller effect. Boxes can also be stored flattened. Boxes that are at least two years old are generally worth between $10 and $30 on the secondary market, regardless of how they've been stored.

Clocks

Time flies when Jeff Gordon races, but you can keep track of it with a Gordon clock! JEBCO, the premier manufacturer of NASCAR-licensed clocks, has an extensive collection of Gordon merchandise. All of the time-pieces JEBCO produces come individually numbered as part of a limited edition series. One AA battery is enough to power their precision quartz movement. In addition to mounted clocks, die-cast replicas of Gordon's famous #24 car also come in the form of an AM/FM clock radio! It's time to add one of these finely crafted clocks to your collection.

Coins

Jeff Gordon collector coins are perfect for any race fan looking for a change. Enviromint, one of the leading manufacturers of collectible sports medallions, has commemorated Gordon with several coins ranging from bronze to pure gold. Enviromint coins are individually numbered and kept to strict minting limits to increase collectability. Trading card manufacturer Pinnacle also issued several Gordon coins that celebrate his achievements. Like the Enviromint coins, Pinnacle coins are available in several varying qualities of metal.

Coolers

Only the coolest of NASCAR fans possess special Jeff Gordon coolers. They come in hard plastic or vinyl, cylindrical or square, big or small. You can get one that comes in the form of a bag or one with a race car for a lid. There's even one from Sports Fan Products that has three separate storage areas. NASCAR is offering a cooler manufactured by Gear as one of the many prizes available in the "NASCAR YOUR CAR" promotion. Get one now while the items are still hot!

Fishing Lures

You'll reel in a winner every time when you use Jeff Gordon fishing lures. Functional lures manufactured by Oxboro Outdoors and fully licensed by NASCAR are vibrant and colorful. One features Gordon's photo and signature, while another is decorated with a picture of his car. Collectors can also find a novelty fishing lure in the size of a 1/144 die-cast of the #24 vehicle. This lure isn't intended to catch you any fish, however – just envious looks from other Gordon collectors. Lures usually cost less than $8.

Hats

Hats on for Jeff Gordon! Gordon hats are extremely popular and widely available. There are a seemingly unlimited number of different colors, logos and designs to choose from: everything from a #24 cap to one commemorating Gordon's three Winston Cup victories. Persistent collectors can also find more unique items, such as leather caps. Most caps have adjustable sizes and can be found at almost any place that carries NASCAR collectibles.

Ice Cream

Satisfy your sweet tooth with a double scoop of Jeff Gordon ice cream. Whether you know the company as Edy's or Dreyer's, the ice cream is made with the same ingredients and mouthwatering flavors. Several limited edition flavors have been offered, including "Sweet Victory Sundae" and "Checkered Flag Sundae." The latest flavor to be found in cones everywhere is "Jeff's Mint Chocolate Sundae," which won a taste test for which Gordon was a judge.

Inflatables

When people tell you that your Jeff Gordon collection is full of hot air, take it as a compliment. They might be admiring your Gordon inflatable car. These cars are available in sizes of 25" and 40", and are produced from high-quality plastic that can withstand even the most rough-and-tumble drivers. There are also Gordon inflatable chairs available. Alvimar Performance Company's seats provide cushiony comfort and include amenities such as beverage holders. You'll be glued to your seat no matter what the outcome of the race is!

Jackets

There are so many different Jeff Gordon jackets available, you could wear a different one each day of the week. From simple cotton twill to exquisite cowhide leather, Chase Authentics makes a variety of jackets for any price range. They even make a Pepsi Racing jacket for the fans of Gordon's Busch circuit sponsor. So whether you favor the bright colors of the rainbow or a more subdued look, a Jeff Gordon jacket has you covered!

Key Chains

These collectibles are especially appropriate for Jeff Gordon fans, because they are meant to be used in your car! More traditional collectors will find officially licensed pewter key chains by Great American Products right up their alley. Fans looking for something a little more unique will want talking key chains shaped like Gordon's car. Gordon key chains are readily available at stores that sell NASCAR merchandise, are inexpensive, useful and widely manufactured. We all know Gordon holds the key to success – it can't hurt to let him hold your keys as well!

Knives

A Jeff Gordon pocket knife is the perfect souvenir for a rugged race fan. A few limited edition knives are priced at several hundred dollars on the secondary market. However, the more conservative collector can get a cut of the action with less of a strain on the wallet. Many knives, including ones with handles in the shape of Gordon's car, can be purchased for under $20 on the secondary market. A legitimate knife will come with a certificate of authenticity assuring the buyer that it is a fully licensed item. Knives can be purchased at racing stores, trackside or on the Internet, and are made by several well-known manufacturers, including Action and Case Racing Collectibles.

Lighters

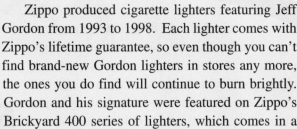

Zippo produced cigarette lighters featuring Jeff Gordon from 1993 to 1998. Each lighter comes with Zippo's lifetime guarantee, so even though you can't find brand-new Gordon lighters in stores any more, the ones you do find will continue to burn brightly. Gordon and his signature were featured on Zippo's Brickyard 400 series of lighters, which comes in a special collector's tin. A Brickyard 400 lighter was produced after Gordon's win in 1998, but it does not feature his signature.

Lithographs

Not surprisingly, Jeff Gordon is a favorite subject among auto racing artists. Lithographs are part of a limited series, which is usually about 500 pieces. Collectors have a number of Gordon lithographs to choose from, and will find the recent-release price of

around $100 or $200 fairly reasonable, especially when compared to prices in the thousands of dollars for an original painting! A lithograph by painters such as Sam Bass or Rick Finn of an exciting moment from Gordon's career can really add class, style, and value to any Gordon collection.

Mouse Pads

Turn the computer area at your home or office into a racetrack with a Jeff Gordon mouse pad. The big and bold "24" will let all your curious co-workers know just who your favorite driver is. Once you've bought the mouse pad, a Jeff Gordon mouse should be your next logical purchase. Shaped like Gordon's DuPont Monte Carlo, the mouse is both stylish and sporty. Just don't let your boss catch you using your mouse to drive laps around the desk! These computer accessories won't take a bite out of your paycheck. A set consisting of a mouse, mouse pad and screen saver costs just under $50. A mouse pad sold by itself will cost you much less.

Ornaments

Christmas is not the only time of year perfectly suited for displaying this handcrafted Hallmark ornament. Featuring Gordon and his car, the ornament is poised to capture the checkered flag. This ornament, released in 1997, was the first in a series that included fellow racing legends Richard Petty (in 1998) and Bill Elliott (in 1999). Like most ornaments, it was only available for one year, so you won't be able to find it on the shelves of your local retail stores. But with the right combination of luck and patience, this ornament can be hanging in your collection soon!

Pins

These enameled pins make the perfect addition to your favorite shirt, hat or jacket. Small in size, but as colorful as the rainbow, they come in various shapes and designs. Even Gordon's Jurassic Park car has been honored with its own pin. These miniature works of art won't poke a hole in your wallet – a set of six can run you less than $20. Don't delay in adding these to your collection – many pins are limited editions so they won't be sticking around for long!

Plush Figures

Both collectible and huggable, plush figures are growing in popularity by leaps and bounds. Gordon fans can find Rainbow Warrior–themed plush bears dressed in T-shirts or driver suits in a number of sizes, shapes and colors. Plush figures also come in the shape of Gordon's car and even Gordon himself! Well-known manufacturers such as Racing Champions, Action Performance and Team Up International, among others, have begun putting these collectibles on the market. They're available at hobby shops, Internet sites and tracks around the country.

Posters

Posters are one of the most popular Jeff Gordon collectibles available. No other product captures the color, speed and beauty of stock car racing quite like a poster does. Posters are colorful, inexpensive and look great wherever you hang them. With just a little searching and a lot of wall space you can find posters of Gordon, his car or his crew to decorate your room. Even the largest posters are still affordable. A giant six-foot tall door poster will only cost you about $15. There are also motivational posters for sale that emphasize teamwork that will inspire any Gordon fan.

Puzzles

It's no puzzle why Jeff Gordon is so popular with NASCAR fans. The first Gordon puzzles were manufactured by Milton Bradley. Today, you can find several jigsaw puzzles produced by Winner's Circle, also known for their quality die-cast cars. Beginner puzzle fans can test their skills on a simple 200-piece puzzle, while more experienced puzzlers can challenge themselves with the Puzz3D series by Winner's Circle. These puzzles let you put together a three-dimensional reproduction of Gordon's DuPont car and are perfect for passing the time on a rainy afternoon.

Radio-Controlled Cars

Deep inside you know you were meant to be the next Jeff Gordon, racing down the track in your #24 rainbow Monte Carlo, hugging the curves and passing the competition on the straightaways. You may not be the next Rainbow Warrior, but you'll feel like him when you race your radio-controlled #24 rainbow car! It takes nerve and skill to control one of these beauties. Battery powered, these cars can go anywhere you can find a track! Speed forward, turn in reverse. The car is made of heavy-duty construction in case you "hit

the wall." You can find radio-controlled cars by toy maker Hasbro at any toy store.

Telephones

A telephone that looks like a die-cast racing car collectible of Jeff Gordon's 1/24 scale Dupont Monte Carlo – how cool is that!? Number 24's rainbow car sits on your tabletop, supporting your loyalty to Gordon while doubling as a functioning telephone. The cord attaches from the back bumper directly to any jack. You speak, listen and use the push buttons from the underside of the chassis. The

headlights flash when the phone rings, the ringer switches from tone to pulse and redial and mute buttons are also included on this racing fan's telephone. Columbia Tel-Com gives new meaning to the term "car phone."

Travel Bags

Soft-sided bags are great when you travel to Jeff Gordon's races. You'll love the convenience of a bag that can squash down into small spaces and then fill to enormous capacities all the while letting everyone know which driver is your hero! You can use them to indulge in your desire to acquire more Gordon memorabilia, because you have the perfect bag to carry it all in. Gordon's travel bags are made of lightweight, water-resistant material and have zippered closures.

T-Shirts

What better way to show your support for Jeff Gordon than to wear it? T-shirts are abundantly available on-line, at stores, and of course, trackside. They come in a rainbow of colors and usually range in price from about $15 to $25. Along with basic shirts featuring Gordon's name, photo and car, manufacturers have also developed more specific designs. Wear them with pride!

Video Games

You can get a taste of the thrill and excitement of racing through Jeff Gordon's XS Racing video game manufactured by ASC Games. On a racetrack located in the future, you compete against worthy

rivals while getting valuable tactical information from the Wonder Boy himself, Jeff Gordon. Once you've blown away your competition, you can match wits against your master, Gordon. Who will emerge the victor?

Watches

For the Jeff Gordon enthusiast who already has more obvious novelties such as shirts and hats, a watch is the next purchase to make! Many different styles are available to choose from – wrist or pocket watch, leather or metal band in many different colors and sizes – and are manufactured by Sportivi, Montana Silversmiths and Sun Time, among others. These watches are worth seeking out at the track, racing collector stores, on-line or through catalogs. Just think – every time you glance at your wrist, you could be seeing Gordon's face, car number or signature!

Jeff Gordon's® Fans Share Their Stories

Jeff Gordon fans are some of the most die-hard NASCAR followers in the sport. From Connecticut to California, NASCAR fans have embraced the heroic driver of the rainbow-colored #24 car. The sport has even begun to take hold all around the globe. Men and women, both young and old, live and die week-to-week on Gordon's fortunes at the race track. These following fans provide a small sampling of Gordon's legion of admirers.

Nevada

Craig of Las Vegas considers himself Jeff Gordon's number-one fan. As someone who originally knew nothing about NASCAR, Craig has gone on to become one of the foremost collectors of Jeff Gordon memorabilia.

Although he is involved in the sports collectibles business, Craig didn't catch the Jeff Gordon bug until 1997. He was shopping in a retail store when the youngster he was with pointed out a Jeff Gordon car and asked Craig to buy it for him. His curiosity raised, Craig watched a NASCAR race the next week and Jeff Gordon won. From then on, Craig was hooked.

Not satisfied with only collecting Gordon's Winston Cup collectibles, he was determined to go back to the beginning of Gordon's career and collect it all. In addition to the 400 die-cast cars now in his collection, he also has stand-ups, plates, race-used tires and unused race tickets. He has met Gordon on and off the track and has had several pieces in his collection autographed. Craig and Gordon have even appeared together on a live QVC program!

Every March, Craig attends the Winston Cup race at Las Vegas Motor Speedway in style by renting an infield space and camping out in a motor home for the week. He is a member of the Jeff Gordon fan club, and was at one time the fan club's regional coordinator for the entire southwest region of the United States. He also shows his support by flying Jeff Gordon and NASCAR flags in front of his house on race weeks.

Ohio

Gino was born and raised in Ohio, where Jeff Gordon used to be a familiar sight at the local tracks, competing in sprint car races. Gino became an early fan of Jeff Gordon, but lost track of his career by the time Gordon had entered the Busch series. When Gordon entered the Winston Cup circuit, however, Gino began collecting Gordon memorabilia in earnest. Pictures and die-cast cars now line the walls of Gino's kitchen. Gino admits his kitchen needs to be 10 times larger for him to fit in everything that he'd like to display. His favorite die-cast is the 1997 ChromaPremier with its distinct gold-and-black paint scheme. Gino's collection is not limited to traditional collectibles. If it has Jeff Gordon's picture on it, you're almost positive to find it in Gino's collection. He also has a large number of other items such as soda cans and cereal boxes that feature Gordon.

One thing you won't find in Gino's collection are cars with special finishes such as gold or silver. He prefers replicas of cars that Gordon has actually driven.

The collectibles he enjoys best are early midget and sprint car items – items that take Gino's memories back to seeing Gordon race on those small, local tracks.

Gino is assembling his collection for his son's enjoyment, also. Although it may be too early to tell what driver will become little Gino's favorite, it's a safe bet to assume he too will become a fervent fan of the rainbow-colored #24 car.

Switzerland

At first, Barbara may seem like your typical Jeff Gordon fan. Like most fans, she took an instant liking to Gordon after watching him race and began collecting die-cast, photos and trading cards of him. What sets Barbara apart from other collectors is that she lives in Switzerland! Stock car racing is not as popular there as it is in the United States, but Barbara did not let that stop her from fol-  lowing the sport. To keep up to speed on Gordon, Barbara became a member of Gordon's fan club and subscribed to "Inside NASCAR" magazine. She acquired many of the pieces in her collection through on-line auctions. Barbara was able to see Gordon in action up close when she attended a Winston Cup race in Las Vegas. Barbara hopes to return to the United States again to see Gordon race in the Coca-Cola 600. Barbara's dedication proves that Gordon's appeal is truly a worldwide phenomenon!

Connecticut

Cindy and her husband Michael have been race fans for years. She has followed Gordon since his rookie year and her three sons Cody, Cory and Chase have joined in the thrill of following their mother's favorite driver. The boys are the true Jeff Gordon collectors

in the family, with die-cast cars, helmets, soda cans, hats and jackets making up their collection. The whole family watches the races every week, and despite the fact that Michael is a Dale Jarrett fan, Cindy and the boys never gang up on him.

Although Connecticut hosts no Winston Cup events, the family has not let that stop them from experiencing NASCAR racing up close. They

have attended races in Daytona and Charlotte with NASCAR-enthusiast friends because there's no thrill quite as great as cheering on your favorite driver in person!

Connecticut

Rob grew up in a family of racing fans, and when he started following an individual driver, he found he could identify with the young, up-and-coming driver Jeff Gordon. Rob's collection took off in 1996 and he has since accumulated a vast collection of 1:24s, trading cards, cereal boxes and more. One of Rob's favorite items is Gordon's Diet Pepsi midget racer.

Rob's hobby is also his job, as he works in a fully stocked race store, Race World. One of the many positives of his job is that Rob is constantly surrounded by great Gordon die-cast items, such as the Jurassic Park Monte Carlo. Despite the job's perks, Rob still has to wait just like any fan for the shipment of new Jeff Gordon products to make the long trip through the mail to the store.

Displaying Your Collection

Most race fans spend considerable amounts of time and money in assembling their Jeff Gordon collections. After all this hard work, it would seem pointless to store your items under a bed or packed away in boxes. Utilize any cabinet and countertop space you have available.

Die-cast cars are the perfect display item when they are lined up in a nice, shiny row. If you have die-cast cars for drivers other than Jeff, you can prepare for race day by organizing your cars in their corresponding starting-lineup positions.

Jeff Gordon apparel doesn't need to be kept away in closets and dresser drawers when not being worn. By placing clothes hangers outside of the closet, you can let everybody see your favorite clothes any time of the year. Other hangers also have practical applications. You can re-create a store display by hanging your 1:64-scale die-cast cars on a rack. This lets you keep your die-cast cars in their original packaging while allowing you to view and admire them.

Don't forget to include Gordon's colors in your display. The colorful rainbow pattern is an important part of his identity. By choosing furniture and shelving in colors identified with Gordon, such as blue and red, the room itself becomes a part of your Jeff Gordon collection.

Utilize as much wall space as you can. Pennants and collectible plates look perfect displayed on the wall. You can also do the same for license plates. Now you won't have to worry about which Gordon license plate will go on the front bumper of your car! The couch is another part of the room just waiting to become Gordon-ized. After all, it's here where you'll spend your time watching Gordon battle for the checkered flag on race days.

Whether you choose to personalize it with a few die-cast pieces or with other mementos is up to you.

Action figures made by companies such as Winner's Circle are an alternative for collectors who want to display more than just cars. Although action figures look impressive in their original packaging, don't be afraid to open one up and place it on your desk, bureau or workbench. Just don't expect it to retain as much secondary market value once it has been removed from its packaging.

Prints and photos look best when mounted and framed on a wall. You can also create your own prints by cutting out pictures of Gordon or his car from magazines and then mounting and framing them yourself. You can do the same for photos that you might have snapped on your trips to the racetrack. If you're really lucky, you might be able to get Gordon to autograph a picture or photo. Although the racetrack keeps him very busy, Gordon often makes public appearances to meet his fans. When people ask you where you bought such a nice print, you can take pride in telling them that you did it yourself!

Trading cards offer other colorful, inexpensive images that can be framed on a wall. Be aware that some Jeff Gordon trading cards are worth hundreds of dollars, so consult the Trading Cards section beginning on page 107 of this Value Guide before you decide to put your potentially valuable cards up on your wall.

Cardboard stand-ups and full-size posters make great conversation pieces in any collection. The only other way you'll ever have a life-size Jeff Gordon in your house is if he shows up on your doorstep and makes a personal visit.

Pit row play sets can be left in, or taken out of, their packages for display purposes. Create an exciting diorama by combining different pit scenes together.

Tires aren't just for your car anymore. You can almost smell the burning rubber when you purchase official race-used tires to add to your display.

Gordon has endorsed several food products over the years, and these colorful containers shouldn't be relegated to the kitchen cupboard. Soda cans are just the right size for stacking and displaying. Although cereal boxes can be either emptied out or left full, you should probably eat all the ice cream before you display one of his Edy's or Dreyer's containers. What a delicious predicament to be in!

Using plastic storage containers is an excellent way to protect and display your larger die-cast cars. These plastic containers are sturdier and offer better protection than cardboard boxes or sleeves. Try stacking these containers in interesting shapes. Just don't stack them too high – they might tip over and collapse on you!

Many of the larger-scale cars can be removed from their original packages without destroying the package. This lets you take them out for display purposes, but retains their secondary market value should you choose to sell them in the future. Placing your die-cast car on top of its corresponding box makes a simple, yet effective display.

Unless you have unlimited space, you probably won't be able to show off your Jeff Gordon collection throughout your entire house. The solution to this problem is to think vertically. Sturdy metal shelves can stretch upward to hold even the largest collections. By keeping your collection above

ground level you also lessen the chance that your valuable die-cast cars will be picked up and played with by children or damaged by pets.

What happens when you run out of wall space but still have more posters in your collection that you want to exhibit? Try tracking down a store display for use in your home. These can often be found for sale by racing stores or individual collectors. If you see a Gordon display piece being used at a retail store, talk to the store's manager. The store just might be willing to part with it when it is done using it. Remember, it never hurts to ask!

A glass display case can lend a showroom quality to your collection. Checkerboard-patterned shelves make the display case even more race worthy. Your local arts and crafts store is a terrific place to shop for supplies to brighten up your displays. What you fill your case with is up to you, but don't hesitate to be eclectic. A mix of transporters, duallies, gas pumps and cars looks terrific when grouped together. Don't hesitate to include both Busch and Winston Cup cars.

You can even include small apparel items such as baseball caps in your showcase. If you receive many Jeff Gordon items as gifts for holidays and birthdays, consider placing all these items together in your glass showcase. Family and friends will love seeing the items they bought for you on display.

The History Of Die-Cast

Die-cast cars have been around for almost a century, but it is only in the last decade that they have truly bloomed as a collectible. Although there have been die-cast reproductions of NASCAR stock cars since the racing days of Richard Petty, the hobby has really seen its star rise with today's superstars.

Manufacturing die-cast cars is a multi-million dollar industry, but it did not become this way overnight. The industry has grown much like NASCAR itself – steadily and enormously.

There are currently several manufacturers producing die-cast NASCAR replicas for a variety of budgets. Whether you enjoy pocket-sized 1:64-scale cars or highly detailed 1:18s, there are several companies to purchase from.

Die-Cast Toy Pioneers

The history of die-cast toys dates all the way back to the turn of the century! In 1893, Charles Dowst saw a Linotype machine at the Columbian Exposition of the Chicago World's Fair. In just a few years, Dowst would use the Linotype process to produce the first die-cast toys. Dowst's company later became known as Tootsietoys.

How A Mold Becomes A Car

Early die-cast toys were made by pouring liquid metal into a mold or die. Less toxic and more affordable compounds are now used in the production of die-cast vehicles, although the basic process remains relatively similar.

The dies used in die-casting can be quite costly, so manufacturers have to make their profit by producing large amounts of product from a single die. Even today, companies will occasionally alter older car molds, rather than produce a whole new mold.

Each car begins as a concept that is then rendered into a drawing. Once the specifications are agreed upon, a prototype is made. This prototype may change several times before production begins. Most companies have overseas manufacturing facilities where the die-cast cars are made using a zinc alloy and plastic components. The base color of the car is usually baked on and then a special tampo process is used to apply the logos. All these steps, and more, must be finished before the completed product is ready to hit the store shelves.

Matchbox® And Hot Wheels®

When people think of die-cast cars, they usually think of Hot Wheels and Matchbox cars before stock cars. Although they have ventured into the world of NASCAR replicas, these companies are more well known for their toy line.

Matchbox cars date back to the 1950s, but their story actually began in 1947 when Leslie Smith and Rodney Smith started Lesney Products. The company started producing die-cast cars after experimenting with other die-cast products. Matchbox would reign as the king of die-cast cars until the arrival of Hot Wheels.

Hot Wheels premiered in 1968. These sleek and speedy cars, made by Mattel, captured the imagination and allowances of millions of young kids. The line has continued to hold its popularity, with over two billion Hot Wheels cars having been produced since 1968.

The rivalry between the two die-cast manufacturers ended in 1997, with Mattel's merger with Tyco Toys, the then-maker of Matchbox cars.

Die-Cast Today

Racing Champions was one of the first companies to whole-heartedly jump into the NASCAR die-cast business. Their 1:64 cars

have been a common sight on toy store shelves since 1989. By distributing their cars through mass-market retail stores, Racing Champions was able to gain wide-spread visibility for their product. While many serious collectors consider Racing Champions as toys and not collectibles, the company has won over many collectors with the introduction of gold-plated cars and the hobby store–exclusive Authentics line.

Racing Champions has recently acquired Ertl. Ertl was another early NASCAR die-cast producer. Darrell Waltrip, Richard Petty and Dale Earnhardt were some of the driving heroes of the early 1980s whose cars were produced by Ertl in 1:25 and 1:64 scale.

Chances are that many of the die-cast cars in your collection are manufactured by Action Performance. Action possesses a sizeable portion of the die-cast market. Brookfield Collectors Guild and Revell were two die-cast giants that are now owned by Action.

Action cars are praised by collectors for their detail and accuracy, with even the 1:64 cars displaying elaborate paint schemes and finishes. Whenever you see Jeff Gordon race a special "Star Wars" or "Peanuts" car, you can thank Action. The company started the whole craze in specialty paint jobs with the idea for a silver Dale Earnhardt car in 1995. The car proved to be a big hit at the racetrack and on store shelves.

Originally, unique paint schemes were unveiled for special NASCAR events such as the Bud Shootout. Now it's not uncommon to see several cars each week sporting a special paint scheme. Although there have been hundreds of specially painted cars raced since Earnhardt's trendsetting ride, they still prove to be a special favorite among fans.

Today, NASCAR and the die-cast world have become even more closely knit. In 1999, the Roush Racing team, known for manufacturing several cars, including those of Mark Martin and Jeff Burton, acquired the high-quality die-cast manufacturer Team Caliber.

Team Caliber is part of the recent trend of companies producing exceptional-quality die-cast stock car reproductions. These cars are far removed from the simple die-cast offerings available for years on toy store shelves. The bar is constantly being raised in terms of quality and detail.

As NASCAR continues to display unlimited growth and potential, the same holds true for the world of die-cast. Both new and old fans of die-cast collectibles have much to be excited about as the die-cast manufacturers and NASCAR work closer together.

Caring For Your Collection

After you have invested considerable time and money into building up your Jeff Gordon collection, you should take proper care of it. You don't want your 1:24-scale die-casts getting damaged and looking like they just crashed into the turn wall at the Daytona International Speedway. Following these simple tips will help keep the pieces in your collection looking as vibrant as they originally did on store shelves.

Caring For Die-Cast

Most cars should remain in their original packages in order to retain secondary market value. A 1:64 car removed from its blister card loses nearly all of its resale value. Larger cars that come packaged in boxes, such as 1:18 and 1:24 scales, can be easily removed from their boxes and displayed without automatically ruining their value.

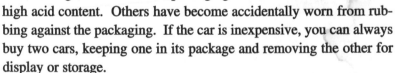

It's too early to tell what long-term hazards might arise from leaving a new car in its original package. Some older die-cast cars have been damaged when left in packaging with a high acid content. Others have become accidentally worn from rubbing against the packaging. If the car is inexpensive, you can always buy two cars, keeping one in its package and removing the other for display or storage.

If you choose to display your larger die-cast cars out of their packaging, you should have a method for storing them. Display cabinets make a wonderful home for your cars. The glass doors on these cabinets let you admire your collection, while keeping them safely protected. If you don't have any extra cabinet space, several companies sell affordable display cases made from high-quality plastic. These cases have compartments for several cars and can either be displayed or stored away.

To remove dust or dirt that may build up on your car, lightly dust it with a soft cloth. Don't attempt to clean or polish it with any harsh or abrasive cleansers. Another danger to your car's finish is bright light. Prolonged exposure to hot lamps, lights or sunlight will fade the paint of your cars. You should also avoid exposing your cars to excessive heat and humidity. Repeated handling of your cars is discouraged. The chemicals on your skin can be very damaging and every time you pick up a car, you increase the likelihood of accidental damage.

Other steps you can take to enhance the appearance of your collection include using mild polishes, glass cleaners or car wax. These cleaning steps should be performed for your own enjoyment, because collectors often prefer cars in their original condition, even if it means a few scratches or a duller finish.

Caring For Trading Cards

Keeping your Jeff Gordon trading cards in proper condition is both easier and harder than caring for die-cast. You will probably never need to dust off your cards, but trading cards have their own

special care tips to keep in mind. Even the slightest tear, crease or blemish on a card will cause its secondary market value to plummet. Luckily, there is an almost endless supply of binders, boxes and sleeves available to protect your cards.

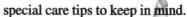

Trading cards suffer a similar fate as die-cast after prolonged exposure to light. Don't store your cards in a hot attic or damp basement, either. A moderate climate is key to prevent the advanced aging of your cards.

When you hold your cards, avoid placing your fingers all over the card. Grasp the card by its edges. This will prevent fingerprints and smudges from defacing your card.

Caring For Other Collectibles

Although die-cast cars and trading cards make up a significant portion of most collections, they are not the only collectibles that need to be cared for. Food items present a particular problem for collectors. Should the contents be emptied or remain in the package? Soda cans and bottles should remain unopened. Open soda containers lose just about all their secondary market value. Other food products, such as cereal, can be opened. Some collectors leave cereal boxes full, while others empty out the food, then stuff the box with newspaper to give it a full appearance. You can also flatten your cereal box and then place it in a protective bag or sleeve, much like you would a baseball card.

As Jeff Gordon continues re-writing the record books, many of his earlier collectibles may become more valuable and tougher to find. Taking the time to care for your Jeff Gordon collection now will save you the expense of having to replace carelessly damaged items in the years to come.

Index

– Key –

All Jeff Gordon die-cast pieces are listed below in alphabetical order by year. The first number refers to the piece's page within the Value Guide section and the second to the box in which it is pictured on that page.

Acknowledgements

CheckerBee Publishing would like to extend a very special thanks to Craig Maraldo, Chris Cozzens and Kurt Kjormoe. We would also like to thank Bruce Breton and Dave Daniels at Collectibles of Auto Racing; Bill Grey, Violet Posci and Rob Riddell at Race World; Gino R. Bidinotto and his friends; the Gabor family and Cyndy Norton. These individuals all contributed their valuable time to assist us with this book.

Catch The Thrill...

CheckerBee PUBLISHING

with our other hot guides!

COLLECTOR'S VALUE GUIDE™

NASCAR®
Dale Earnhardt®
Jeff Gordon®
Wrestling
Hot Wheels®
Beer
X-Men®
Fifty State Quarters
Harry Potter™
Ty Beanie Babies®
Pokémon™

And that's not all! We have 27 great titles available in stores everywhere. They're action-packed! To find out more, call toll free:

800.746.3686 or visit CollectorBee.com

It's Racing Excitement

If you're a fan of Jeff Gordon, our web site is for you! Check it out today!

CollectorBee.com

- Keep up with the latest NASCAR news!
- Meet other racing fans on our free Bulletin Board!
- Try your luck with our contest & giveaways!

306 Industrial Park Road   Middletown, CT 06457   800.746.3686   www.collectorbee.com